Welcome

THE
EVERYTHING®
PARENT'S GUIDES

A s a parent, you're concerned about your child's growth and development, and you want to ensure that your child grows up happy and healthy. THE EVERYTHING® parenting books are there to guide you along the way, answering questions, dispelling myths, and providing important information from various experts, pediatricians, and other medical professionals and seasoned parents.

The Everything® Guide to Raising a One-Year-Old and *The Everything® Guide to Raising a Two-Year-Old* books are specific guides that take you through your child's various stages of development. This specified series covers crucial topics pertaining to growth and development, emotional development, day-to-day issues, family life, recognizing and rewarding good behavior, avoiding and dealing with bad behavior, learning, nutrition, safety, common illnesses, potty training, and even play time.

The Everything® Guide to Raising a One-Year-Old and *The Everything® Guide to Raising a Two-Year-Old* books are an extension of the successful parenting books in the EVERYTHING® series. These authoritative yet accessible books will help you navigate every year of your child's life, so you can rest easy knowing you have the resources to ensure your child's health, happiness, development, and overall well-being—giving you more time to concentrate on what matters most—your child.

Visit the EVERYTHING® series at *www.everything.com*

The
EVERYTHING®
Guide to Raising a Two-Year-Old

Dear Reader,

This book is intended to help you understand better the fundamentals concerning your two-year-old's health, development, and personality. But first, a hint of what we believe is the best thing you can do during this period of your child's life: not worry! Our aim in writing is for you to enjoy your toddler, particularly by recognizing that children at this age are a natural source of pleasure.

We have two essential observations to relay about two-year-olds. The first is that they have a sense of humor. Although infants will laugh when tickled or when they see someone else laughing, two-year-olds actually laugh at funny things, such as when their mom or dad is acting silly. They even do funny things on their own.

The other delightful discovery to make about two-year-olds is that they are in love with life. No doubt you've already experienced that if you wake up in a bad mood and your two-year-old wanders into the room— little footed pajamas drooping, carrying a favorite stuffed animal—your blues instantly lift. Two-year-olds are so gosh darn cute! Their faces and pint-size toddling bodies simply bring joy to a home.

It is in this spirit that we invite you to look more closely at your child's second year.

Brian Orr, M.D.

THE

EVERYTHING®

GUIDE TO

RAISING A
TWO-YEAR-OLD

From personality and behavior to nutrition
and health—a complete handbook

Brian Orr, M.D., and Donna Raskin

Adams Media
Avon, Massachusetts

To all parents with young children — Brian

• • •

*This book is dedicated to my father, Art Raskin, who when I was a little
girl smiled at me again and again. Thank you for that. — Donna*

• • •

An Everything® Series Book.
Everything® and everything.com® are registered
trademarks of F+W Publications, Inc.

Published by Adams Media, an F+W Publications Company
57 Littlefield Street, Avon, MA 02322 U.S.A.
www.adamsmedia.com

ISBN 10: 1-59337-728-2
ISBN 13: 978-1-59337-728-1

Printed in the United States of America.

J   I   H   G   F   E   D   C   B   A

Library of Congress Cataloging-in-Publication Data
Orr, Brian G.
The everything guide to raising a two-year-old / Brian Orr and Donna Raskin.
p.   cm. — (An everything series book)
ISBN-13: 978-1-59337-728-1
ISBN-10: 1-59337-728-2
1. Toddlers. 2. Toddlers—Development. 3. Child rearing.
4. Parenting. I. Raskin, Donna. II. Title.
HQ774.5.O744 2007
649'.122—dc22
2006028212

*This book is available at quantity discounts for bulk purchases.
For information, please call 1-800-289-0963.*

THE

EVERYTHING
Series

EDITORIAL

Publisher: Gary M. Krebs

Associate Managing Editor: Laura M. Daly

Associate Copy Chief: Brett Palana-Shanahan

Development Editor: Rachel Engelson

Associate Production Editor: Casey Ebert

PRODUCTION

Director of Manufacturing: Susan Beale

Associate Director of Production: Michelle Roy Kelly

Cover Design: Erick DaCosta, Matt LeBlanc

Design and Layout: Heather Barrett,
Brewster Brownville, Colleen Cunningham,
Jennifer Oliveira

Acknowledgments

Thank you to Donna Raskin. You are dedicated to the task and easy to work with. And thank you to my family—Bernadette, Patrick, Ailene, and Theresa—for allowing me the extra time to write this work. You are my pillars of support.

—Brian

•••

Thank you to Brian for being the best collaborator I could work with, as well as being a wonderful doctor to my son. Thank you, too, as always to Paula Munier, who mothered three children while managing to be a good friend and a great editor to boot. That's not easy! We also thank Kate Powers for her editorial skills.

—Donna

Contents

Introduction

By the time your child is two, you probably can't imagine living without her. After all of the demands thrust on you with having a new baby at home, taking care of a toddler is a bit of a treat. Now you have a funny, interesting little person who keeps you company, is happy to help you out around the house, and wants to learn and do as much as she can. Two-year-olds are fascinated by life and are curious about everything, which makes them not only eager learners but fascinating companions.

By the end of your child's second year, he will understand hundreds of words and will start to prefer certain activities over others. As his personality develops, the two of you will begin to form a truly interactive relationship. He'll accompany you on errands, becoming aware of and even coming to depend on his daily schedule (so that he may not like it if the schedule changes). If he's in day care, he'll also learn to trust in and rely on his teachers as well as begin to form friendships with specific children.

Of course, there are those other, darker, moments when your little angel stops smiling and turns into what seems a completely different child. Such times always seem to erupt when you're out shopping, visiting a grandparent, or in any public place where you're liable to become embarrassed.

As you will learn in this book, the reassuring news about these difficult moments is that they are common to all parents. In fact, a two-year-old's bouts of frustration and sudden outbursts are a normal phase of development; the less agitated you become in response to your child's behavior, the less intense her tantrum will be. In other words, don't sweat it! This book will teach you how to acknowledge your child's feelings of frustration without providing so much attention that you encourage more tantrums.

Despite the sometimes-trying moments that are bound to occur as you devote time and energy to raising your two-year-old, it is important to keep a few things in mind. Two-year-olds are a wondrous combination of baby and child, of being both cuddly and dependent, on the one hand, and of excitedly asserting whatever independence they've carved out for themselves, on the other. It's fascinating to watch your two-year-old learn and grow, all the while becoming a strong individual within the family. Enjoy this second year with your child, remembering to have fun with each other as all of you learn and grow as a family.

Chapter 1

The Myth
of the Terrible Twos

M ore than any other stage of a child's life, that of the "terrible twos" worries many new parents. The description of this period as terrible traditionally refers to the two-year-old's penchant to say "No!" and to demand that things go exactly the way the child wants. And although such petulant behavior can create problems for both parent and child, it marks an important stage in your child's development: the achievement of a budding independence. For, in reality, this second year is a remarkable time indeed, centered around a curiosity-driven recognition of one's self and of the development of interests.

A Notorious Stage

Before the age of two, your child develops from infant to toddler—he is by now halfway to preschool! In order to negotiate this transition successfully, he needs to become accustomed to a sense of himself as an individual rather than as still a baby who is attached to you. Of course, the conflict that arises for a two-year-old is that just as he is discovering himself as an individual, he comes face-to-face with reality—he needs adults to help him with just about everything. In fact, many psychologists as well as parents have compared two-year-olds to teenagers, for at each stage of life the child is trying to separate from his parents and yet continues to rely on them. And for both parent and child that conflict entails a struggle. This dichotomy is especially frustrating to a two-year-old, who has neither the language skills to communicate his inner tension nor the ability to contain his frustration.

Toddler Independence

A toddler's attempts to try out independence involve a number of new skills she is developing, such as talking, moving, and learning. For example, she may want to speak the way you speak (and so ends up saying "no" a lot). Feeling increasingly in control of her body, she may seek out the freedom to run wherever she wants, to climb up high, or to hit a ball with a bat. She may not want to go to bed (especially if you're staying up late) or to be told what to eat.

At first glance it might seem as if your toddler is trying to break the rules, but in actuality she doesn't quite know the rules yet. She sees you doing certain things and doesn't understand why she can't do them. Sometimes she is not allowed to do something because it isn't safe, sometimes because it's against the rules, and other times because she lacks the ability without realizing it. But she only learns such distinctions through trying. You are the person who will end up guiding her through most of these experiments.

 Fact

Believing that you can succeed in reaching a goal through your own efforts is known as self-efficacy. You can instill in your child a sense of self-efficacy by giving him encouragement as he goes out into the world. By seeing the results of his efforts to attempt something, your child learns something significant.

Walking away from you in a store, demanding to have oatmeal for breakfast, wanting to wear his favorite T-shirt even though it's dirty—a toddler asserts his new independence through whims and spontaneous desires. But though you see the big picture (he could get lost in the store; he had oatmeal for breakfast *and* dinner yesterday; the T-shirt is dirty), once he has set his mind to something, he has a hard time letting go of the idea.

Depending on your response to your two-year-old's behavior, either a power struggle might arise or, alternatively, he could feel empowered and cared for. In short, if you focus on making your child feel reasonable in his desires all the while you are setting rules and boundaries, you will avoid most tantrums and manage to get through the day smoothly.

Celebrating Independence

It is important to recognize that your child's desire to do something by his own initiative isn't intended to slow you down or disrespect you. He simply wants to do something he finds interesting, and he isn't aware that his desire might interfere with your plans, be dangerous, or be something he's not ready to do. So first acknowledge—respectfully—what it is that he wants to do.

Once your son understands that you're there to support him, offer him assistance or suggestions based on the situation. Sometimes you might just want to step aside and assess how he does on his own. Rather than solving a troublesome problem for him, explain what's going on and see if he can figure out a solution.

For example, let's say your son wants to make his own bowl of cereal. You watch him go to the refrigerator and take out the milk. "Hey! Are you going to make your own breakfast? That's great!" you call to him. He's carrying the milk carton by the top but rather than take it away from him without explanation, you go over to him. "Let me show you how to carry that," you say, putting his hands on the bottom of the carton so he can hold it more firmly.

After he puts the milk on the table safely, he opens the pantry door to get the cereal. It's on a high shelf. "I have an idea!" you say. "How about if we put all the cereal boxes on the bottom shelf so you can reach them?" You move these down so that now he can make a choice. He chooses the sugary treat rather than the low-sugar pick, of course, but you don't say a word.

 Essential

> Your child feels proud of himself for trying new activities and being able to do them. He wants you, too, to appreciate his growing mastery of the world. No matter the result of his efforts, try to praise your child's attempts at independence. This will make him feel confident and capable—necessary qualities to take into the world.

These steps continue until you are able to say to your son, "What a great job you did!" Afterward encourage him to help you clean up.

Temper Tantrums

There's always a chance that your child's assertion of independence and her testing of limits will come together in one hard-to-handle eruption of anger and frustration. That uncontrolled outburst of emotion is what we know as a tantrum. Tantrums, which can be physical, verbal, or both, look like fits: Your child may scream, cry, flail around, and altogether seem unable to calm down. These outbursts are difficult to handle because they often come on suddenly and make your child seem as if she's become some child you've never met before. Where did your lovely sweetie-pie go?

Two-year-olds are easily frustrated because they want to do things that are sometimes too hard for them. They may want to swim in the deep end of the pool or ride on the grown-up roller-coaster. On the other hand, some two-year-olds are easily frightened by new experiences or by their parents leaving the room. Fear and frustration are two of the most common causes of tantrums because they are two of the most common feelings two-year-olds experience.

Tantrums involve emotions and behavior, two areas in which parents don't have control over their child. Your child needs you to identify her emotion for her and then to help her cope with it. "I see you are angry. I've been angry, too. Here's how to help yourself. You see, I'm not angry anymore." The more reassuring you can be for your child, the more likely it is that she will look to you for help.

Tantrums are often cyclical. Your child may have a few in a row or it may seem as if in an entire month you don't remember a day when there weren't tears or screams. If your child—and you—are stuck in this unpleasant cycle, consider taking a break from each other for a day. Do something for yourself and let your child spend the day with her other parent, a grandparent, or a friend. And don't sweat it if she behaves better for them than she does for you! Chances are the break will bring you back together with both of you more relaxed.

Exhaustion Tantrums

A child may have a tantrum for a number of reasons and there are different types of tantrums. Your child may become easily frustrated with himself, annoyed with a toy, or be so tired or wound up that he can't stop crying. When you sense that the tantrum is likely the result of exhaustion, take your child to his bed, to a couch, or perhaps into the car, encouraging him to lie down and relax. Even if he's crying or yelling about something seemingly unrelated to being tired, such as insisting on having a special toy, reassure him that he just needs to take a break and calm down.

When a tantrum is less about physical exhaustion and more about behavior, a few things can provoke it—a desire for attention, anxiety over an impending separation, a struggle for power. It may simply be because your child is testing where the boundaries for proper behavior are. Is he allowed to scream? Is he allowed to hit? How far can he go with this behavior? Your answer needs to be swift and clear: not far!

Acting out is a term that describes emotionally based behavior, and it occurs at any age, even in adulthood. For example, overeating can be acting out if you're not hungry but are instead feeling angry or lonely. If your child is having tantrums out of the blue, it's possible that something not immediately apparent is bothering him. Ask him once or twice if something is wrong. Even if he can't tell you or you can't think of a cause, don't allow his behavior to become an impediment. Frequent tantrums are not okay, no matter what is causing them.

Coping with Tantrums

When you find your child losing it—crying uncontrollably, hitting, or throwing things—get down to his eye level, gently put a hand on his arm or back, and speak softly to him. It's very possible that your calm reaction will calm him down. Even though you may want to yell or respond to his emotion with emotion, in most cases that won't work. Nor will slapping or spanking him. He will then be upset over two things: whatever first bothered him, and the fact that you have hurt him. Even if he stops crying, it is likely because he is afraid of your reaction. His subdued response doesn't mean he has learned anything useful. All he has learned is that you are someone who will hurt him.

 Fact

Temper tantrums are upsetting and embarrassing for parents. If your child has one, you'll wonder what you did wrong to cause this behavior. And if you're with friends, family, or in public, you'll feel like you're under a microscope. In these situations, walk somewhere with your child, even if you have to carry him out of the store or a room.

First, validate your son's experience by saying something like, "I see you're really upset." Then explain that you are not angry at him and show that you are there for him by saying something like, "I want to help you. But I need you to calm down and take a breath so we can figure out how to fix the problem." Depending on your child's personality, you might want to keep talking or simply stay with him, showing him how to take a deep breath and how to relax. You can smile, look into his eyes, and basically take him out of his emotional state. Alternatively, you might need to ignore the behavior. If your child thinks he can control you with his tantrums, he will keep having them.

Although it may seem perhaps too sensitive to respond so calmly to your child's outburst, you need to remember that, most likely, your child doesn't want to behave badly. In fact, he is probably as surprised by his own behavior as you are. If you are calm and help him understand that he can feel aggravation and frustration but not act out those feelings through inappropriate behavior, he will learn there is an alternative.

Language Frustration

At two, your child doesn't know how to recognize, express, or solve her frustration. Even though she does understand more than she used to, in some ways having grown up a little actually exacerbates her frustration. When she was one, if something upsetting happened she came right to you. Now that she's two she wants to fix the problem, but she can't.

Worst of all, she doesn't have the ability to explain any of this to you. Tantrums are an opportunity to teach your child how to deal with frustration and intense, negative feelings—feelings that are a reality in life. She needs to learn how to handle and express anger without resorting to unacceptable behavior.

 Alert!

During a tantrum, you may need to restrain your child so that he doesn't hurt himself. Kneel behind him and wrap your arms gently around his body so that you're holding his arms down. Speak softly in his ear. Take deep breaths, as he may begin to breathe the way you are breathing, and that will help him relax.

If you weather the tantrums successfully (for, rest assured, there will be more than one), your child will come out on the other side with the ability to express his feelings instead of acting them out. Instead of hitting, crying, or yelling, at least most of the time, he will say, "I'm angry you're not buying me that toy!"

Emotionally intelligent adults have learned how to recognize their feelings and then how to cope with them. If you are tired, you lie down when you can; if you are angry, you might talk your feelings through with someone. But children have yet to learn how to make a connection between a problem and its solution. Tantrums are a way for a child to discover how to handle his emotions so that, as he grows up, he's less likely to be overwhelmed by them. He starts this learning process by listening to himself and then by verbalizing his needs to others.

Ignoring the Tantrum

In some cases, the best response to a child's tantrum is no response. If you have tried to help your child calm down but she is simply unable to stop crying or yelling, try walking away (this can work if you are at home). That will both help you remain calm and communicate to your child that her behavior is not going to get her any added attention.

In fact, not engaging with your child's high-intensity emotions is one of the most effective parenting techniques for managing tantrums. Show your child that you care and that you are nearby if she needs you; then let her know you will only give her attention if and when she can behave calmly and respectfully.

Tell her where you'll be ("I'll be in the kitchen while you stay in your room" or "I'm going to sit over on the couch"), and then give her time to compose herself. You can check on her every few minutes so that she knows you haven't truly left her (remember, two-year-olds can easily get scared about being abandoned), but don't keep asking her how she is. Take the focus off her behavior.

She may tell you that she can't calm down. (This is probably the truth, as she has yet to learn how *not* to let her emotions run away with her.) Explain that you will help her calm down. Show her how to take deep breaths and how to relax her body. The point is to attend to her only when she's focused on feeling better and not when she's yelling or out of control.

Setting Limits

Many people assume that children don't like rules. In reality, children appreciate and thrive when clear, well-established boundaries are set on what they are allowed to do and how they should behave. The most effective limits are reasonable, clear, and are explained before the rule is likely to be broken. In other words, try to convey what is expected before your child is in a testing situation. If you're going to a store, say, "I'd like you to try to stay near me and not run off. Also, I expect you not to shout when we're in the store."

Your child will not remember all of your rules, nor will she be able to follow them consistently and without reminders. However, if you remind her of them and if you enforce them consistently, she will get used to limits. She will even appreciate having distinct rules to follow that guide and temper her behavior, especially if social outings become more harmonious as a result.

Helping Your Child Abide by Limits

Rules should be specific. "Be nice" is not as helpful as "Say please and thank you" or "Ask, 'May I be excused?' before leaving the table." Also, the limits set should be framed positively. "No hitting!" is much less effective than "Keep your hands to yourself."

If your child breaks a rule or needs help with his behavior, before you admonish him be sure to give him a few warnings, calmly accompanied by an explanation of what consequences he'll face upon misbehavior. Parents institute various policies on when exactly they step in with enforcement. Some parents, for example, will give two warnings before disciplining.

There are several ways to deal with rule-breaking by a two-year-old. First, you can give him a time-out, whereupon he has to sit for two minutes. (The rule is a minute for each year of age.) A time-out need not be for a set time period, nor does it mean that a child has to be alone. It is simply a period in which a child receives no attention and is unable to issue demands.

It's often advisable to use this tactic when your child isn't interacting well. You can say, for instance, "We don't hit," as you take him away from disturbing another child. You might subsequently let him sit with you, but communicate only minimally with him. Allow him instead to calm down on his own. After a minute or so ask him, "Are you ready to play properly?" He'll tell you when he is. Time-outs only work if they happen immediately after the infraction and are short. (If one lasts too long, your child won't remember why he's even sitting there.)

 Fact

> Your child can help create rules with you. When you are heading out to a relative's, ask her how she would like to behave. She may be able to say "Be nice" or "Say thank you," and you can build on those sentiments. Be sure to acknowledge how wonderful it is that she came up with such a positive idea.

If your child behaves badly, you can also try to warn her of a specific consequence that will result if she doesn't stop the behavior. If she's shouting in a store, for instance, you can take her outside and explain that if she continues to yell you won't buy her the toy she wanted.

Consequences cannot be idle threats. They have to be realistic, enforceable, and such that the punishment fits the infraction. If your child is throwing a toy, for example, it is appropriate to take the toy away for a few minutes, but not to make her stop a play date by taking her home.

Choosing Your Battles

Everyone breaks rules. Sometimes it's more important that your child develop a sense of self-determination and discerning judgment than to blindly follow orders. In fact, children sometimes follow rules too closely and will hold you to ones that aren't always appropriate for adults (such as not being allowed to bring a drink into the living room).

Your child will feel a little thrill when you break a rule with him—say, if you bring soda into the living room or let him have a cookie before breakfast. You will not lose your authority if you are able to demonstrate how rules are, in the end, flexible.

Now, what will you do when your daughter breaks three rules in a row? She throws a toy, yells, then, a few minutes later, brings her sippy cup into the living room. Do you respond to all three or pick one?

You should probably pick one and let the others slide. Your daughter is only two; she's likely to remember one rule but not three rules at one time. Pick the most egregious problem and talk to her about that. Try not to react to the whole scene, which would be too much information for her and, further, could make you sound more critical of her than of the particular behavior (which may affect her self-esteem).

Sticking to Routines

One of the most effective ways to limit the potential for tantrums is to establish and stick to routines as much as possible. Routines help children feel secure by giving them a structure to rely on. When children know what events to expect because their daily routine is familiar to them, they are more easily able to learn how they are supposed to behave at most times and in most situations.

Eat, Sleep, Play

Two-year-olds are always busy: They play, explore, and interact with you and the world around them. Some activities, such as sleeping, mealtimes, and play time, need to occur on a set schedule. If you create a schedule around these daily events, you'll find that you have time to do things for yourself.

 Essential

Whether your child has a nanny, goes to day care, or stays at home, you can use the following suggested routine to create a schedule for her day. Fortunately, day care centers typically follow a schedule that they stick to reliably. If they don't, try to find new day care, because routines are important wherever your child spends the day.

At two, your child is probably napping once during the day, for a longer period now than she used to. So start planning the day around that information, because reliable naptimes can really help a child to feel good and have energy throughout the day. Even if your child refuses to nap, set aside an hour or two of downtime to allow her to rest, if not to fall asleep.

Then figure out your meal times based on naptime. Do you want your child to eat an hour before her afternoon nap? Do you want her to eat soon after she gets up and then go a few hours until dinner? Answering these questions will give you some basis for how to plan your day.

Play time, errands, cleaning, and the rest of your to-do list can be scheduled around naptime and meals. Be sure your child also has some unscheduled time to play each day, whether at home, on a playground, or at a friend's house. Once you schedule all of these activities, chances are you'll find time to accomplish what you need to do and you may even come to rely on this routine.

Why Routines Work

Routines work not just for children but for parents, too. That's because everyone in the family follows different timetables that need coordinating. And though you don't want to be too strict about sticking to your own schedule—after all, children have their particular rhythms and sometimes will nap for a longer or shorter period than you expect—you will feel calmer if your day goes according to plan.

As emphasized previously, daily routines provide children with a much-needed framework. Time designations are difficult for them to put in perspective ("later" or "two o'clock," for example, are abstractions to a two-year-old), but even two-year-olds are able to remember the pattern to regular events day after day. A child knows, for instance, what to expect when you tell him, "It's naptime." A two-year-old's body becomes accustomed to a daily rhythm, which helps your child's moods and energy levels stay steady and reliable.

Discipline Basics

Until your child turns two, you probably don't think about discipline issues very much. Now all of a sudden, when your child frustrates you or seems to be misbehaving on purpose, you find yourself reacting the same way your parents did in similar situations—you yell, you walk away, or you spank your child. Or maybe you behave in the opposite way of your parents. If they spanked, you become quiet instead. If they yelled, you try time-outs.

Discipline is different from punishment and it is very different from an impulsive reaction to a behavior. Discipline is something you teach and your children learn. It is not a response, but the understanding that you are guiding your child's behavior so that she can eventually adapt and internalize your instruction.

 Alert!

Punishment is authoritarian and teaches that a more powerful person has control. Punishment does not instruct. Punishment also assumes that the child has done something bad, as opposed to doing something he hasn't yet mastered. Effective forms of discipline use consequences that teach a lesson or that are in line with the misbehavior.

Rather than paying attention to your child's negative behavior, single out positive behavior of his that you can praise and give attention to. If you only pay attention to negative behavior, your child will feel insecure. By contrast, if you notice and compliment his positive behavior, he will respond in kind with continued good behavior. In other words, negative behavior should be responded to quickly and with as little attention as possible, whereas positive behavior should be rewarded with more attention.

Sharing Your Child's Perspective

Although they are more aware of rules than one-year-olds, two-year-olds do not break rules intentionally nor do they purposefully try to manipulate their caregivers. Because two-year-olds want your love, approval, and care, it would not occur to them to do something to jeopardize that.

On the other hand, two-year-olds want what they want when they want it, and this will naturally put them at odds with your agenda.

Staying in Control

There is no question that being a parent can be frustrating and exhausting. Constantly having to monitor a small child's behavior is a hard job. When a child is being unreasonable and out-of-sorts, it is often very difficult not to lose your temper and begin responding to her yelling and crying in a similar fashion.

Moms and dads lose their tempers. However, you need to follow (at a bare minimum) the same rules you are setting for your children: no hitting; no out-of-control yelling; no throwing; no name-calling; no being mean.

Sometimes losing your temper is not the worst thing in the world. You are a person with boundaries and limits, and children need to see that there is a line they shouldn't cross. However, when you do lose your temper (this often takes parents by surprise, so it's actually hard to stop beforehand), do your best to keep your voice at a reasonable volume and explain to your child that you are losing it.

Then do what you need to calm down: Walk away for a minute; have a glass of water; take a few breaths; make a phone call. It can be a valuable lesson for your child to watch someone calm herself down after losing her temper.

Finally, afterwards, explain to your child what just happened to you, letting her know that you are a person who needs to be treated well, just as you treat her. Your child will understand this and appreciate the concept of fair play.

Detaching

Successful parents bond with their children in a very deep and meaningful way, which gives the parent-child relationship a foundation of empathy and an emotional intensity. Almost all of the time this bond is positive and valuable. Sometimes, however, especially when a parent is stressed and a child is overly cranky (or when a parent is busy and a child is being obstinate) the closeness becomes an implosion. In other words, the child begins to melt down and the parent, who may have something else on her mind or may have been pushed too far, also gets upset.

When this happens, it is beneficial to simply detach. Let your child have her tantrum; let her cry; let her be miserable for a half-hour. Having a bad moment or even a bad day is part of life. Even though you are her parent who loves her more than anything else in the world, that doesn't mean you also have to have a bad day.

This intentional detachment can feel unsettling to you as a parent after having created such a close relationship with your child over two years. As a result of your intense bonding, you probably aren't fully aware of just how much you have allowed your child's mood or emotions to become part of your own mood and emotions.

A case in point: Say your two-year-old is having a tantrum at the mall. Put her in the stroller, ignore her behavior, and take care of yourself. If she's crying too much to stay in the mall, take her somewhere else you want to go. Or bring her home and turn on the TV to something you want to watch. Obviously you want to make sure she is safe, but other than that, you can feel good about taking some time to improve your own mood and your own day.

Chapter 2

Growth and Development

Your toddler changes a great deal during this year, even if he doesn't grow at the same rate as in the previous twelve months. He will come to speak completely for himself (knowing some 300 words by his third birthday), to run around, and attempt to hop, skip, and jump, if he isn't doing this already. He will cry less, have more patience, and probably have fewer fears. The world will be more familiar to him.

Developmental Milestones

At twenty-four months, your child likely is more squat than long and his balanced center of gravity helps him walk. As the year proceeds he will thin out, gaining inches though adding only between two and four pounds.

Your child undergoes many physical changes this year. He becomes able to kick a ball and to look behind him as he walks. He may even try walking backward. He enjoys riding a low tricycle and swinging on swings. Such activity gives him a sense of what his body can do and how it feels to move in different ways.

 Fact

Young children ask "Why?" frequently because they are curious about the world. Suddenly they start to notice things they didn't before: The sky is blue! Mommy goes to work! Daddy likes to listen to music! Answer your child's questions as entirely as possible without getting too wordy or deep.

Encourage your child to undertake new things, such as to drink from a grown-up glass (just fill it a little in case it spills), to carry something while he walks, thread large beads on a string, button his coat, and build with blocks.

The Toddler Mind

At the age of two, your child is actually starting to make connections based on what he's learning and experiencing.

For example, when he sees a horse at a farm and realizes it resembles his toy horse, he may comment "Horse says *neigh*" or "Horse like mine" rather than simply pointing out "Horsey!"

Because of your child's new understanding, he comprehends what you mean when you tell him, "We're going to the store later" or "I need you to bring me your sweater, then go in your room and get your coat." At the end of this year, he will seem more like a little person than a baby.

The Toddler Personality

Your two-year-old by now exhibits a distinct personality, even conveying particular preferences. When she wakes up in the morning, she recalls a toy she wanted to play with the previous evening. She chooses favorite books to bring you to read and has particular friends she prefers to play with. She asserts her opinions and expects you to respect these.

Although your child's personality is still forming, in some ways it has already established itself. You probably have noticed characteristic ways she responds to new experiences and to frustration, and what her overall temperament is. As you help her learn how to help herself and how to do her best, you want her to feel good about herself.

Physical Skills

Some of your child's most impressive physical developments during this year might seem small—she becomes able to thread beads, to hold a crayon properly, to play with little toys, and to turn pages in a book. Your child may start to pull pants on and be able to stir using a grown-up spoon. While the majority of physical growth occurs before the age of two, with your child's change from baby to toddler the finer points of physical development now manifest themselves.

Before he turned two, your toddler's gait was a side-to-side one, but as this year progresses he starts to walk forward with bigger and longer steps, as well as to walk backward. He relies less on his hands to go up stairs and holds onto railings with more confidence.

Your son's balance also improves, to the extent that he is able to stand on one foot and to move about in various directions. Whereas previously his dancing took the form of an up-and-down, knee-bouncing motion, you now might see him twirling around as he dances.

Language Development

Conversations with your child become more elaborate as he begins to construct sentences more correctly. He understands place words—such as *under, on top,* and *behind*—and uses these properly. And he understands feeling words, too, such as *sad* and *funny.* Sometimes he'll even astonish you by uttering long, complex phrases.

Just as when your child was learning his first words, speak to him as you would to an adult. There is no harm in using grown-up words to a small child; it will in fact expand his vocabulary. Continue reading to your child to build his vocabulary.

Sometimes it feels funny to be talking continuously to your two-year-old, but such running commentary really helps a child connect words to experience. "Okay, now I'm going to start dinner. I need to get the meat out of the refrigerator and start to boil the water," you say as your son bangs on pots and pans on the floor. He looks up at you and some of the new words start to make more sense.

 Essential

Encourage your child to ask questions, explaining that questions are a way to learn more and to find out answers. If you see that your child doesn't understand something you've said, ask, "Were you wondering what that word means?" Or, when you don't understand what he says, feel free to say, "I don't understand. Can you repeat that?"

Stuttering and Lisping

Even the most articulate child stutters and lisps a bit. Some letter sounds, especially those pronounced with the lips together such as *p*'s and *s*'s, are difficult for a child to master (*d* and *t* sounds are the easiest). Thoughts are a challenge for a two-year-old to get out in speech as quickly as she thinks them. Lisping is particularly noticeable when a child uses a word with blended letters, such as *bl* or *sp.* So, for example, *block* might be voiced as *bock* and *spoon* as *poon.*

Don't worry, though. Pronouncing words clearly is not the norm until a child reaches the age of five. Stuttering and lisping by your two-year-old is developmentally appropriate—a natural stage of speech development, in other words. All you need to do is pronounce a misspoken word back to your daughter properly, in a natural manner. So if she says, "My bock tower is big!" you can reply, "Yes, your block tower is big."

Mispronunciation

As excited as you are by your two-year-old's complete sentences, you may notice that "the doggie is brown" sounds more like "da doggie iz bwown." To some extent this mispronunciation is a physical challenge, since as his tongue and mouth are still adjusting to working properly. To your child, the words he's speaking sound the same as yours, which is just fine. You needn't correct his pronunciation, since all that matters at this point is that he's constructing sentences and communicating by means of them. His speech will undoubtedly improve over the next year or two. The fact that you and the rest of your family are able to understand him is what's important.

Normal Growth

When you take your child to the doctor, the doctor will weigh her and measure her height, then compare this reading with a growth chart to determine whether your child is growing appropriately. Her weight and height will be compared with those of children her age to establish what percentile she falls in.

Most children grow on course, and it really doesn't matter what percentile they are in as long as they thrive and develop. When it comes to percentile ranking, being in a higher bracket isn't necessarily an accomplishment, nor does such a result automatically predict how big or small a child will be when she grows up. As long as good, nutritious food is provided to them, children will eat enough to grow well.

Boy–Girl Differences

One of the surprising discoveries made over the last twenty-five years is that, given equal opportunities and treatment, boys and girls nevertheless appear to be very different in some respects. Such differences, of course, don't mean better or worse by comparison, simply that boys' and girls' development is often marked by traits and preferences that seem related to gender, rather than to differences of personality, ability, or capability.

 Alert!

If your child seems to be having more trouble speaking than he should, it's possible that someone other than you—such as a teacher—will notice. You understand him, but if they can't, they can sometimes hear the problem. Many schools and communities now have specialists to help small children with their speech.

Although your daughter likely plays with dolls and your son with cars, there are, of course, plenty of social exceptions to these norms. One of the most supportive and loving things a parent can do for a child is to look at him without gender expectations. As a result he'll feel free to explore all aspects of his talent and personality without being hampered by a parent's notions of what a boy or girl should be.

A growing body of scientific evidence indicates that the differences between boys and girls stem from variations in hormone levels and the effects of this on brain development. These differences—which include variations in size and structure of the hypothalamus and in brain pattern functioning—though not extreme, do seem significant enough to account for slight variations in gender development. For example, boys tend to develop certain skills such as walking and talking later than girls, and girls tend to be more independent. Once boys are past preschool, their physical bodies will become stronger and better at athletics while girls will excel at school. Whether these differences are because of the way school is organized or because of innate abilities is a question that remains to be answered.

Socialization

Your child at two is more likely to engage in social interactions with siblings and other children than when he was younger. He plays with them in a more friendly way, now offering his toys as well as wanting to do what the other children are doing. Children at this stage begin to figure out in groups and with friends what behavior works and what doesn't. Along the way they experience acceptance and rejection, as well as cooperation and disagreement.

During this year, your child will need you to explain how friendships and play dates work, but you will also need to let him find his own way with other children. A two-year-old wants to act grown up, especially around older children, and wants to do what he sees other children doing, even if it's a little too much for him.

Though you might worry that he's bitten off more than he can chew, keep in mind that his willingness to challenge himself is a good thing! If he feels capable and competent, he'll focus on the many new things he wants to try rather than notice any age differences.

Independence

"Me do it!" Even if this willfulness on the part of your two-year-old may slow you down, the words should be music to your ears. Your child has begun to realize that she enjoys doing things for herself and she now wants to try to do things she couldn't do before. Moreover, she wants you to see—and acknowledge—how capable she is.

 Question

My two-year-old wants me to do everything for him. Should I?
Your son may want to reassure himself that you will still take care of him, or he may doubt his own abilities. Ideally you would try not to become frustrated with this behavior. Instead encourage your child to do something with you, saying something like, "I'll button two buttons; you do the rest."

At the same time that two-year-olds feel good about buttoning their clothes, feeding themselves, and playing with a friend, they also start to worry that perhaps you won't want to take care of them anymore. Or perhaps they will worry that they won't need you. It's almost as if they have become teen-agers—they want you there to cheer them on but don't want you to think they need you. This ambivalence scares them, and they get a little needy as a result.

Your approach to this confusion should be calm and dispassionate. Recognize that two-year-olds have to go through this process to feel good about developing their independence. As they do, they will realize that you are still their parent, there for them no matter what.

Chapter 3

Parenting Issues

If it's not one thing, it's another. Just when you think you have the bedtime routine down, your daughter stops eating any vegetables. Just when she's eating well, she starts having tantrums. Parenting is an endless challenge. Armed with information, however, you can feel confident about tackling the challenges that parenting brings.

Bedtime

There are two important rewards in store for you as the parent of a two-year-old. First, you'll feel proud each time you help your child meet a challenge. Second, you'll come to recognize that child-rearing problems come in phases. With this perspective comes a realization that handling difficulties with love and understanding is far more effective than becoming worried or anxious.

If you have developed a daily routine, your two-year-old is now used to bedtime; she understands what's supposed to happen even if she doesn't necessarily want to go to bed. If she doesn't want to go to bed, it's usually because she has learned that life goes on even while she's asleep. Suddenly she very much wants to stay up with her parents or siblings, or else she is absorbed in whatever she's playing with. Maybe she has a fear of monsters in the closet or something under the bed. She wants to tell you about her fear and have you reassure her.

 Alert!

If your two-year-old resists going to bed, realize that the problem might not be bedtime, but the transition from play and the day to sleep. Rather than abruptly turning out the light, experiment to see if the transition has been too sudden. Perhaps your child needs something altered or added to her bedtime routine in order to make it more appealing.

Sometime during this year, your toddler will be moving into a bed, if he hasn't done so already. The more positive and enthusiastic you are about this transition to sleep, the more your toddler will follow your lead. If he is having trouble staying in his bed, give him some responsibility for it. Ask him to put his stuffed animals back on top each morning or to pick out clean sheets. Toddlers respond well to your belief in their abilities, because they want to be independent and to show off their skills.

Establishing Routines

Bedtime routines help children become relaxed and ready to sleep. In advance of this routine, it is helpful to give your child some time to get used to the idea that bedtime is approaching.

 Essential

Transition from one activity to another is often difficult for two-year-olds because they become committed to the first activity and are not enticed by the prospect of the next one (no matter what it is). You must acknowledge and handle transitions so they don't become issues themselves.

It's a good idea to tell your child that it's almost time for bed about thirty minutes before he needs to start getting ready. Don't announce "Time for bed!" and immediately take him into the bathroom to brush his teeth. Instead say, "It's time for bed in a half-hour," followed by suggestions for (and help in) finishing up the activity he's involved in. If it's a continuing activity, such as block building, offer to keep the project as it is overnight so he can return to it the next morning.

It's very important to respect your child's play time. Just as you aren't able to drop whatever you're doing at a moment's notice or to immediately put it out of mind, you need to help your child get used to the idea of postponing his play and returning to it later.

Once the transition is made—and he will need your help moving through it—then you can begin your bedtime routine, which should include, of course, washing up or a bath, brushing teeth, and a diaper change.

Babying Time

Just like a younger baby, a two-year-old needs a bedtime routine that features snuggling, listening to a story or looking at a book, and singing a song or two. Visualization, discussed in the following section, can help your toddler get to sleep when the bedtime routine ends.

As active and independent as your two-year-old is during the day, there is a good chance she will rediscover her babyness at night. While she may run all over the house (and the store and the park) during the day, for example, at night she'll want to be held. And though she might want to dress herself in the morning, she may insist she can't get her pajamas on by herself at night. Just as being tired can contribute to a toddler having a tantrum, it can also prompt less dramatic changes such as whining, wanting to be picked up, and needing more hands-on care.

Visualization

If your child has trouble falling asleep, try a relaxation technique in which you verbally describe a scene to your child that is calming and relaxing. Try to make the scene as evocative yet as soothing as possible.

For example, ask your child to close her eyes and imagine the scene you are describing to her. Use as many descriptive words as you can. Turn the lights down, lie next to her, and speak very softly, using your imagination to create a scene that is comforting to her.

Try something like this: "It is a sunny day, and you are walking on the grass, feeling warm and tired. The grass feels nice and cool under your feet. The clouds are moving across the sky, and you watch them. One puffy cloud goes by, then two. And in the background you can hear some ocean waves."

Use a scene that will make your child feel good, describing a setting such as a beach, a park, or a lake, or even conjure up a make-believe scenario, like walking through a castle where princesses live.

This kind of visualizing helps young children go to sleep by putting them in a meditative state. The story makes them forget that they're supposed to be trying to fall asleep.

Books and Music for Bedtime

When your child was younger, you probably were reading him very short books in which you pointed out shapes, colors, and other identifying pictures. Now your two-year-old can listen to short stories. He will especially appreciate reassuring stories (such as "The Runaway Bunny" and "Guess How Much

I Love You") that help him go to sleep knowing that he is loved and cared for. In addition, the sing-song style of writing in storybooks helps lull him to sleep. See Appendix C: Books and Toys for Two-Year-Olds for suggestions.

Many two-year-olds also like hearing a song or two before they go to sleep. You can put music on for your child—there are lots of CDs created specifically for this—or you can choose a special song that you sing each night before turning off the light.

Naps

As discussed in Chapter 1, most two-year-olds take one long nap during the day. Sometimes, however, your child, may need a second shorter nap or some downtime at another point in the day. A two-year-old needs about eleven to fifteen hours of sleep a day, and most two-year-olds don't sleep for a long enough period to get all of this sleep at night.

 Question

I'm at my wit's end because my daughter doesn't sleep. Help! Talk to your pediatrician. Sleep is one of the issues doctors get the most questions about, and they often have creative solutions (many suggested by other parents). They may be able to give you sound advice, even if the issue is a behavioral rather than a medical problem.

There are two types of people: larks and owls. Larks are energetic and happy in the early morning, whereas owls take a while to wake up and are at their best later in the day, often at night. This internal clock is something we're born with. You will find it easier to keep your child happy if you work with her natural clock rather than trying to get her to stick to an artificial schedule.

If Your Child Resists Napping

Many parents find that their two-year-olds resist getting into their cribs or beds during the day. If your child is like that, you might need to come up with a creative solution, such as taking her for a stroll and letting her continue to nap in the stroller after you return home, or going for a drive and after she falls asleep, transferring her to a bed back at home. You might also allow your two-year-old to nap in your bed, which will feel special to her and less like *sleep*.

If your two-year-old is still waking during the night, you can take a daytime nap with her. This will allow both of you to get some needed rest. Many two-year-olds are in day care, where they usually rest or nap at prescribed times during the day. Children in day care are usually so stimulated and busy that they easily fall asleep at naptime. Another bonus: Their daily schedules usually make it easy for them to fall asleep at the same time each night.

Effective Naptime

It is helpful for your child if her long nap is in late morning or early afternoon so she has lots of time to play between naptime and bedtime. If your two-year-old is sleeping too much during the day, make sure there is a big difference between the amount of light in her room when she's asleep and when she's awake. Keep the house quiet and dark while she's napping and then, wake her up slowly with light, music, and the sound of your voice.

If your two-year-old is having trouble sleeping at night, you can also try letting her do a quiet activity with you rather than having a second naptime. This will allow her to relax without actually sleeping, helping her mood to stay even during the day.

Wake Time

One of the most effective ways to ensure that all sleep times are truly restful is to make sure time spent awake is energizing and lively. Your child should always have some time outside every day: Fresh air is good for everyone. Also, she should be able to run around and play no matter what else is going on around her.

Sometimes parents have to become adaptive about ways to entertain and keep their two-year-olds engaged during the day. The following suggestions aren't everyday solutions, but they are good one-shot ideas for when you and your child are both tired of being cooped up:

- go bowling (many places have special lanes for children)
- go to a museum
- go to the library
- go to a movie
- walk through a neighborhood

If the weather or the size of your home prohibits either time outside or an indoor space where your two-year-old can be active during the day, consider going to the mall, a toddler play-time program (sometimes held in gyms or YMCAs), or even to an indoor public pool. It is impossible for anyone to sleep well at night, especially a two-year-old, if her daytime isn't stimulating.

Fears

The fears of a two-year-old are very much tied to his imagination. His fear of the dark, of thunder and lightning, or of strangers is exacerbated by the images that arise in his mind. For example, the dark might conceal monsters, the thunder might be someone's anger, and strangers might be people who want to hurt him.

Discovering the Sources of Fear

The most important thing to do when your child is afraid is to get him to talk about his fear as much as he can. Ask him for details. What does the monster look like? What does your child think the stranger will do with him? Although this may seem counterintuitive (if you don't talk about something, you might think it will go away), the reality is that the more open your child is about his fears and concerns, the more able he is to see the fear as irrational and unlikely to come to pass. This is true even for two-year-olds.

Further, taking the fears of your child seriously by listening to them with respect will show him that you care about him and are validating his experience, which is a necessary component of trust.

When he is expressing fear, a child may really be asking his parents, "Should I be afraid?" By listening to him, you can show that you respect his fear. At the same time, you are actually conveying that he shouldn't be afraid. You are showing him that you believe what he says he is experiencing, but you also know more about the situation than he does. This communication encourages your child to trust you.

The Unknown World

Your two-year-old may also be apprehensive about the social world you're slowly exposing him to. At two, there is a good chance your child will be going outside more and meeting new people. She is expected to interact more with new people and to answer their questions. "How old are you?" they will ask. "What's your name?"

 Alert!

Try not to respond in place of your child. Even if she's shy, let the situation play itself out as long as possible. It's easy to jump in and answer questions for your child, but if you do that too much, she won't get used to having conversations with new people. She'll also come to think that it's your job to speak for her.

Before you go to a new place or take your child into a new situation, explain to her what she can expect. Remind her of the people she's going to see: "Remember Aunt Gloria?" "We went to her house last year, and you had fun!" Describe what she can expect: "We're going to have dinner, but first you'll be able to play with your cousins Julia and Audrey. They have a big swing set outside."

If you know of something that might make your child fearful, say, a dog or a relative who tends to be loud, warn her about this. "Uncle Peter has a big dog named Brooklyn. He barks, but they're going to keep him in the garage while we're there; you won't see him, but you'll hear him."

If your child does get scared or worried, reassure her calmly about the situation and tell her that it's okay to feel scared by new things. The more comfortable you feel with the situation, the more comfortable your child will feel. Don't shrug off her fears, because these are very real to a young child. Your two-year-old needs to know that her feelings of apprehension are valid and that she can look to you for reassurance.

Spoiling

A spoiled child is one who is self-centered and demanding, which to many people defines the two-year-old personality. So how do you differentiate between what is normal two-year-old development and what is spoiled-child behavior? Moreover, how do you make sure your two-year-old doesn't grow up to be a spoiled fourteen- or twenty-year-old?

Spoiling and the Two-Year-Old Personality

Spoiled people believe their needs are more important than anything else, even if what they feel as a pressing need is actually a want. Spoiled people have yet to learn they are not the center of the universe and instead see themselves as the star of any given situation. Since this is absolutely the natural point of view of a two-year-old (which doesn't necessarily change until a child becomes a teenager), a good parent understands that this is a developmental stage. Nevertheless she expects her child to learn how to wait, to be patient, and to communicate his needs without acting spoiled.

You can spoil a two-year-old with too much undeserved attention, with too many possessions, and with not enough attention. Too much undeserved attention means giving false praise ("You're the smartest baby ever!") or praising when instruction would be more useful ("You almost carried the milk to the table! That was great. You're wonderful!" rather than "That was a good try. Next time, use both hands to hold the cup, and I think you won't spill anything.")

 Essential

Love—acceptance, affection, and support—does not spoil a child. You cannot love someone so much that they become spoiled. What spoils a child is a lack of boundaries, a lack of explanation about what's going on in any given situation, and a quick response to any demand, no matter how silly or meaningless it may be.

Owning too many things is a problem because children then begin to expect presents every day and at every outing. Worse, they begin to seek constant novelty and never look deeper at what they already have.

When a two-year-old's basic need for attention is unfulfilled, he may resort to overly dramatic behavior—whining, crying, yelling, and screaming—to get what he needs. A child whose parent neglects him or doesn't offer support and reassurance will find a way to get attention and validation. Often that means acting out inappropriately.

Teaching About Gifts

Your two-year-old probably does not ask you for too many things. Even so, you'd do well to be aware that the way you treat gifts, gift-giving, and buying things for your child at this age affects how she behaves in stores in regard to new toys when she gets a little older.

Nowadays you (and your child's grandparents) can buy toys in all kinds of places, even at the grocery store or a gas station and not just at a toy store. This situation sets up children so that they are constantly being bombarded with different new toys. It's important to restrain the urge to think your child is better off with lots of toys. Instead, from an early age let him get used to the idea that gifts are special rather than everyday treats. If he gets used to that at two, then he won't expect to get every new item he sees in stores or on TV commercials as he gets older.

Setting Limits

Although children—and two-year-olds, in particular—want to explore their independence, they don't want endless freedom. In fact, boundaries help a child feel safe and to better understand how to behave as well as what to expect in the world.

The limits you set should be thoughtful and flexible. You should be able to explain the reason for the limit ("I want you to help me put away the puzzle because you took it out and played with it"). At the same time, you should be able to explain why sometimes you are letting the boundary slide ("I can see that you're really tired, so I'm going to put the puzzle away for you. Next time you'll be able to help me.")

This framework will work for many categories in which you need to set limits—establishing parameters for behavior, schedules, the buying of treats, eating, and sleep.

Thumb Sucking

Thumb sucking is normal before the age of four years, so there is no reason to pay attention to it now, especially if your child is tired, sick, or stressed. However, if you think your two-year-old is stressed about something, certainly take the time to discuss this without mentioning the thumb sucking.

However, if your two-year-old is sucking his thumb because he's bored, try to distract him. Give him something to do with his hands, again without alluding to his thumb sucking.

Thumb sucking is an activity that some children are just born to do. Although only 3 percent of children continue this habit past the age of two, the American Dental Association advises that a child can probably suck his thumb until he is four or five years old without damaging his teeth or jaw line.

If someone says something that may hurt your child's feelings when he is sucking his thumb in public (such as, "What's that thumb doing in your mouth?"), go over to him and hold his hand or take him away from that person. You needn't acknowledge the person's rudeness (since you don't want to teach your child to be rude to a stranger). On the other hand, your child needs to know that you are on his side and that you love him just the way he is.

 **Alert!**

Trying to discourage your two-year-old to stop sucking his thumb most likely sets up a power struggle that you will lose. Controlling someone's thumb and mouth, even that of a toddler, is virtually impossible without physical restraint. So offer alternatives to thumb sucking rather than trying to discourage it directly.

Biting

Biting and other aggressive behavior are completely normal for a two-year-old. Nevertheless, such aggression is upsetting to everyone involved, including the child doing the biting. It is important to keep in mind that biting at the age of two is not the same as biting at four, because the two-year-old biter isn't acting aggressively on purpose.

There are some *nevers* when it comes to handling biting. Never label your child *a biter*—biting won't always be a problem since eventually the biting will stop. Never bite back. Also, never give your two-year-old too much attention as a result of biting—if you do, you're encouraging the behavior as a way to get attention. After you help the child who has been bitten, let your child who did the biting see that it doesn't pay to hurt someone.

Biting is just one of many behaviors that two-year-olds try out. Granted, it is one of the more challenging ones and can be particularly difficult to handle when it erupts during a tantrum, but this is not a behavior that will continue very long.

Why Biting Is Common

Typically, the two-year-old biter is frustrated or angry. Given her inability to calmly articulate her feelings rather than act them out, when she finds someone's body part in front of her, she bites without thinking. It is an impulsive action.

Even at two, however, your child often feels embarrassment and remorse for biting someone. In spite of her regret afterward, however, she will defend her right to bite because she feels she had reason to be angry.

Ways to Eliminate Biting Behavior

If you notice two children having a disagreement over a toy, make sure they aren't too physically close to each other; proximity influences whether another person gets bitten in the surge of a child's impulse. Encourage your two-year-old to express her anger through words rather than by means of aggressive actions if she is upset, explaining that no matter how she feels, biting and hitting are never allowed. Do not overreact or dwell on the matter for too long, because attention functions as a reward to a two-year-old. Reassure her that you know she will learn not to bite again, so that she knows you have an expectation she has to live up to. And be patient. At the age of two it takes time and perseverance to change behavior.

Sibling Rivalry

Siblings can be the best of friends and the most intense of enemies. They are helpful to each other, yet they can become sneaky and mean at the drop of a hat. Even though sibling love is often as strong as the bond between parent and child, siblings have to live under the same roof and so have many daily details to negotiate, even when they are little.

Encouraging a Natural Relationship

If your two year-old is about to become a sibling, don't force positive feelings on him. Instead, tell him the news and express your enthusiasm for the new baby. Let your child know that you still love him and that you are looking forward to being a bigger family. Then accept your child's feelings as they come. These will range from positive to negative (fear, anger, jealousy), but if you accept them all, it's more likely the negative feelings won't linger.

Parents need to remember that siblings have their own separate relationships, and that parents can't control how two personalities interact. The more a parent tries to force a good relationship, the more difficult it is for that relationship to develop naturally. While you can certainly encourage kindness and support among family members, you have to allow your children to find areas they have in common, to work out differences, and to create a relationship that works for them.

Motivations for Competition

If two children (or a group of siblings) are arguing, it could be about any number of issues. It could simply be a typical problem such as, "I want that toy, and I don't want you to have it," or it could be about something bigger. Remember, siblings are sharing a lot—physical space and parents, for a start—and sometimes that sharing is too much for a child.

 Fact

> If your children are arguing without hitting, let them work it out. When they tell you why they are angry and why they each think they are right, tell them you don't want to hear it and that you know they can work it out. The more attention you pay to their fight, the more they will try to engage you.

If you notice your children seem stressed over sharing your attention, give each of them some separate time with you. Find a way to play with each one for a while. If they are fighting over sharing their toys, separate them if you can. And make sure each knows he has some toys and possessions that belong exclusively to him.

How to Minimize Rivalry

One of the gifts of having a sibling is the opportunity to learn the art of disagreement. It may sound surprising—parents dread the sound of their children arguing—but the reality is that siblings almost always manage to work out conflict, an essential skill to learn in life.

When your children are getting along and playing well together, you should let them know how happy that makes you. Your approval doesn't have to be excessive, but you can smile at them or just say, "I feel so good when we're all having fun." Offering attention when something good happens is not only self-perpetuating (your children will try to stay good to get more of the favorable attention), it feels better to the parent, too. Wouldn't you rather offer love and support than criticism?

Chapter 4

Common Challenges

You know your child better than anyone else. You know to hand your son his stuffed animal puppy or his blankie when he's tired and waiting for dinner. You know he doesn't like to go to the doctor, so you sing his favorite song as you drive there. Sometimes it seems the best part of being a parent is how connected you feel to your toddler and how well you know how to make him happy.

Comfort Objects

Most two-year-olds have an object with which they have a special connection, often a blanket or a stuffed animal. This object, known as a transitional object, reassures them, helping them to feel safe and secure. Remember, your child has yet to internalize a feeling of confidence, a quality he eventually learns from you. Until then, transitional objects are especially helpful at trying moments, such as when your child is getting used to a new situation, when he needs to relax, or when he is processing a new experience.

The Benefits of Comfort Objects

Because a comfort object is helpful to your child, you shouldn't discourage its use. In actuality it helps your two-year-old make a transition from needing you to comfort him to being able to comfort himself. As a matter of fact, you can feel comfortable offering this object to your child whenever you notice him looking upset or tired. Take care of it for him the same way you take care of things that mean a lot to you. Keep it clean, since he'll probably put it near his face frequently, and always make sure to bring it along before leaving with your two-year-old for a friend's house or day care.

Comfort Objects and Emotional Development

While transitional objects aren't essential for all children, they play an important role in the emotional development of a child. In carrying around his special stuffed animal or his blankie, in other words, your child is transferring the assurance and love he receives from you to the object, imagining that it too has the magical power to soothe him. Even more, he is learning to take the love and assurance carried by the object and give it to himself. If you remove the object, tease your child about it, or discourage him from using it, he will no longer have a useful tool for learning how to comfort himself.

 Essential

> There are a lot of books for children about stuffed animals and blankies, including *Corduroy* (by Don Freeman), *D.W.'s Lost Blankie* (by Marc Brown), and *Blankie* (by Leslie Patricelli). These books will help your child feel it's natural to rely on an inanimate friend.

Avoiding Bad Habits

Most parents think of their children as perfect, particularly two-year-olds, who are relatively new to the world. So how is it that children grow up to become adults with bad habits? When you stop to consider all the behaviors adults do that they wish they didn't—smoking and drinking, eating too much, not exercising enough, being lazy about work, watching too much TV—two realizations arise. First, usually your child will not behave in such self-destructive ways unless an adult in his life gives him the opportunity to do so. Second, with your help and guidance, your child has a good chance of growing up without developing any of these bad habits. Granted, you're not worried about him smoking and drinking at the age of two, but watching too much television, eating poorly, and other harmful habits can develop early in a child.

How Bad Habits Are Formed

Children pick up most bad habits from the adults around them. Children of smokers are more likely to smoke; children of overeaters to overeat. If you want to help your child, you would do well to break your own bad habits. That's not easy, of course, but often parents find they can break an unhealthy habit simply because they are inspired to set a good example for their children.

It is wise to create good habits to begin with. As best as you can, strive to teach your two-year-old habits that will benefit him over a lifetime, such as eating well, being active and not sedentary, and taking care of himself. As a general rule, it is far easier to develop a good habit than it is to break a bad habit.

If you have created a situation in which your two-year-old insists on eating unhealthy foods or does not go to bed willingly, there is a process to follow that can help you break the bad habit. First, don't blame your child for indulging in the habit. In fact, don't make him aware that he even has a bad habit. Don't say, for instance, "The food you eat is terrible!" or "You never go to bed on time!" At the age of two your child doesn't even know what a habit is, so bringing it to his attention only makes him think you are declaring an unalterable fact. He will assume that what you are saying about him is a fixed reality. Worse, he will sense by the negative tone of your voice that something is wrong with him.

After taking responsibility for your two-year-old's habit— since, after all, he is under your control—you are the one who needs to break it. If your child has been eating unhealthy food, you need to provide him with healthy food. If he isn't going to bed easily, you need to create a bedtime routine that works.

 Fact

Rather than being angry at your child for poor behavior, rejoice in the fact that you have control of the situation. When you have control, you possess the ability to solve the problem.

Think positively by concentrating on creating good habits. First focus on which good habit you want your two-year-old to follow. Does he need to eat more fruit? Does he need to be in bed a half-hour earlier? In that case, create a plan to make this happen. Perhaps his morning snack could be a banana. Or maybe you need to shut the TV off earlier in the evening and start reading a book to him instead. You don't have to point out the change to your child. Instead, simply start enacting it.

Finally, be consistent and stay calm. If your child doesn't eat the banana, offer him an apple the next day. If he gets upset that the TV is being shut off, let him cry it out and then show him some books to read. Don't get upset, and don't give up. After a few days—at most, a week or two—the new routine will be the new reality and your child will have completely forgotten about having insisted on the cookies or the TV. Two-year-olds have short memories. The less you make an issue of the situation, the more confident he'll be that the food you've provided him or the bedtime you set for him is the way life should be.

Avoiding the Development of Bad Habits

Two-year-olds often behave in ways that put them in control, even if that isn't their intention. For example, when they yell, scream, refuse to eat, or run away from your grasp, they aren't consciously trying to make you give your attention over to them, although that is the effect. Suddenly it seems they are the sun in the center of the universe, and you are orbiting around them.

It's important to recognize that you are firmly in control of your two-year-old. Don't let his behavior become the epicenter of your attention. Your child eats what you give him; he sleeps when you put him to bed or won't go to sleep if you don't. If you don't put TV on, your child will not watch it; he will go for a walk if you take him for one.

There are moments when you forget you are in control, of course, just as there are moments when your two-year-old rightly should be the center of attention. It is perfectly natural for him to be the focus of certain activities during part of the day. However, it is helpful neither to you nor your child if his emotional behavior begins to run the show.

Even if your child throws a tantrum about the food he is offered or the TV shows he isn't allowed to watch, it is important you make decisions based on what is right for his health and development rather than what suits his mood and emotions. Although it takes time and energy to make sure that your child eats well or to shut off the TV at appropriate times, remember that the habits you create today will stay with him throughout his life.

 Alert!

> Knowing that you're in control is different from being controlling. Although you should take comfort in the fact that you are raising a child, you should also understand that your child needs to grow up feeling in charge of himself. Offering choices to your child and asking his opinion will give him a vital sense of power.

Maintaining Flexibility

However, even good intentions sometimes go awry. If following the day you buy your two-year-old a fast-food hamburger, he refuses to eat the food you normally cook for him, or after watching hours of Disney movies he screams until you turn on the DVD player again, you're familiar with how quickly a child can find ways to get what he wants.

First, you need to steel yourself, promising yourself you're going to wait your child out. If he's refusing to eat, know that eventually he will eat what you give him; if he's screaming, eventually he will stop yelling. Second, even as you explain to your child why he can't have what he's insisting on, you need to offer alternatives.

It's very important that you offer your two-year-old background information on why it's not good to eat too much candy (it makes you overweight; it gives you cavities), watch too much TV (it makes you overweight; it puts you in a bad mood), or not clean up (you won't be able to find your toys when you want them).

Eventually your child will have to make decisions for himself about candy, TV, and other potentially bad habits. The more you entrust him with information in advance, the more likely he'll make the right decisions for himself.

In just a few years he really will be able to listen and understand what you are telling him. He'll remember the instruction you've been giving him and be more likely to remind himself of what's good for him.

Teaching Manners

If you have been saying *please, thank you,* and *you're welcome* consistently to your child, there is a good chance she has already begun using those words herself. Two-year-olds don't always remember the polite words you'd like them to use, but they are familiar with them and understand them.

Two is the age at which your child begins learning manners from you, such as not to interrupt people or to keep her voice down. All the while, be realistic in knowing that most children at two can't yet control all their behavior. As you remind your child about proper behavior, recognize at the same time that two-year-olds aren't capable of being polite under most circumstances. Nevertheless, your setting an example of good manners by modeling politeness and respect for your child both offers her behavior to emulate and prepares her for social interaction in the future.

Demonstrating Good Behavior

You'll want to teach your two-year-old how to eat neatly, how to speak to others politely, and how to remain calm and quiet in most situations. That's a lot. So try to give instructions judiciously and without bombarding her with too much information. If you correct your child too much and too often, she may end up feeling self-conscious. Though it's often difficult to give your two-year-old instructions without seeming as if you're constantly correcting her, there are ways to do it.

 Fact

When playing pretend, you have an opportunity to demonstrate good manners to your child. "Look, the doll wants to ask the horsey if she can ride him," you can say. "Horsey, may I please ride on you? I can? Thank you so much." "You're welcome," the horse says. Your two-year-old will absorb the lesson in this nonstressful scenario.

You could say during dinner, for example, "When I eat, I try to keep my mouth closed because I don't like looking messy when I eat," rather than commanding, "Keep your mouth closed when you eat!" Or you might remark, "I really appreciate that Grandma bought you a nice coat; I'm going to make sure I say thank you in an extra-special way," instead of pointing out, "You forgot to say thank you to Grandma for the coat she gave you." This approach is a form of teaching rather than of leveling criticism.

Instead of expecting your child to speak for herself, understand that most two-year-olds need you to be their mouthpiece. Rather than saying to your child at the end of a play date, "Say thank you to Mrs. Pagano for the nice day you had," you can say in front of your two-year-old, "Jill and I want to thank you for such a nice day. We really enjoyed playing in your backyard." This way your child won't be put on the spot, and she will appreciate being part of your good manners. She will learn that saying nice things to others also makes her feel good.

Offering Praise

If your child squeaks out a *thank you* or remembers to say *please* or *thank you* without being reminded, let her know how good you feel when she is polite. As always, paying positive attention to good manners rather than singling out poor behavior will pay off in a couple of ways. First, your child will be happy you noticed how well she is doing with adopting grown-up behavior. Since independence and doing activities by herself are quite important to her, she will appreciate having her behavior praised.

Second, your child will invariably want to repeat behaviors that get positive attention. So the more you praise what she does that's good, the more likely she'll do it again.

Enjoying New Experiences

Some children are cautious, some are reckless, and most fall somewhere in between. Of course, you never know with any new event if your child is going be brave or panicked, happy or worried. However, there are some things you can do to help your two-year-old get used to new experiences no matter what his personality or mood.

First, remember that whatever your child feels—whether excitement or fear—is acceptable. There is no one right way to feel about a new experience, so don't criticize the way he feels. Instead, keep some fundamentals in mind so that no matter what your two-year-old is feeling, he can come through the new experience feeling comfortable with his natural response.

 Essential

> Even if your child has been to his grandma's twenty times or been to the indoor pool just as often, he may all of sudden become afraid. It's important to remember that even though your child has been somewhere many times before, that doesn't mean he'll recall having been there or what it was like.

The functioning of a young child's memory is not fully understood, either by researchers or parents. No one really knows when small children begin to become familiar with people, places, and things that aren't part of their everyday lives. In the mind of a young child, familiar experiences are always being challenged by new information and the need for new cognitive skills, which can be both overwhelming and confusing. There are a few things you can do to help your child feel better about new experiences.

Preparing for Something New

First, always give your child plenty of information about what he can expect in advance of an activity. Each morning at breakfast or while you're in the car, relay to him the plans for the day. No one likes surprises, least of all two-year-olds. Your child will come to rely on you for these explanations, which will help him start to understand what to expect. Also, as he gets older your two-year-old will begin to remember many of the events that comprise his usual day as well as be able to ask you questions about the various activities ahead.

So you might say, "Today after breakfast we're going to the dry cleaners, the library, and the grocery store. Do you remember the last time we went to the library? We got the book about puppies. Then at the grocery store we're going to buy bananas and apples."

You probably engaged in this kind of running commentary when your toddler was an infant because it helped develop his language skills. He began to learn words from all the different experiences you shared with him. You can continue this dialogue now since it helps him become familiar with the daily routine. Eventually he'll start to anticipate certain events.

Enjoying New Experiences Together

Once you arrive at each place or get together with each person that is part of the day's plan, you'll need to repeat all of the information you've given your child, even if you feel like a broken record. Your two-year-old actually will love these reminders and support. Unlike a four- or five-year-old, in fact, he won't tell you you're repeating yourself.

You can supply your child with more details (compared to when he was younger) about a specific event on the agenda. "Now that we're at the mall, we're going to get you some new socks, and I'm going to look for some pants," you say.

If your plans change in the course of the day, you should acknowledge such to your child, explaining what the change consists of as soon as possible. Some children react very strongly to a change in schedule, but if you give your two-year-old notice along with an explanation, he is less likely to be upset.

Once you've finished with each of the day's activities, you can give your child a little summary of how everything just went—focusing on the positive. "You did great at the mall! I really liked the socks we got and thank you for letting me look at the pants."

Remember, your child has no idea what's right or wrong in this new world you're exposing him to. He doesn't know how people act in malls, what it's like to buy socks, or to look at pants. You are educating him in the ways of the world. By giving him helpful information you are facilitating his making sense of the world, with the result that he feels secure about his place in it.

Enjoying the Company of Your Two-Year-Old

Two-year-olds are natural bundles of happiness and optimism. They wake up eager to dress themselves, and they want to enjoy their daily activities fully (including meal times and doing errands). Parents in the past used to see the natural behavior of a two-year-old as problematic, assuming that a child who wanted to dress herself and took her time doing it was being stubborn or trying to gain some power over her parent. Nowadays parents along with experts know that two-year-olds aren't born manipulators. Rather, they are simply being two—learning, growing, experimenting, and trying to be more grown-up.

If you remember to emphasize mutual enjoyment, particularly when your child is insisting on having her own way, you may find this attitude can help you deal with such behavior more effectively—as well as more happily.

 **Alert!**

If you find that you and your two-year-old have gone more than a day or two without experiencing a lot of fun, let go of your agenda and simply try to enjoy your time together. Don't follow a schedule. Focus on physical interaction and play rather than on instruction and setting a good example.

Parenting is a hard job. Part of that job is to teach your child that following rules, being considerate, and behaving as a member of a family is work. In order to make the work easier for both you and your two-year-old, try to find the fun and joy in whatever you're doing. This will foster a good attitude in your child as well as help make what can be a tedious job for you more entertaining.

If you want your daughter to help you clean up, for example, find a way to make this a game. You could see how many pieces of clothing she can drop into the hamper or ask if she can sort toy trucks and blocks. If you need her to stop yelling, speak so softly that you're whispering and then, when she leans in close to hear you, tell her you've turned into a mouse and want her to be a mouse, too. If you want her to sit quietly for a few minutes so you can talk on the phone, ask her if she'll baby-sit one of her dolls for you.

In other words, with the objective of making sure your child maintains her good humor while she's growing up, you need to be more imaginative than simply saying *No!* all the time. Instead, strive to keep the smile on your child's face at the same time that she's learning the rules of sociability. If your child knows that you enjoy her company and respect her, she will try harder to meet your expectations regarding her behavior.

Maintaining Perspective

As a parent, you no doubt know that two-year-olds can be whiny, annoying, and—well—babyish. It's not always easy to be the only grown-up in the room, especially when the other person is two. Even though you're striving to have fun, to be lighthearted and not squash your child's spirit, there are inevitably moments when you're simply proud you haven't stormed out of the house in frustration. It is during these times that you must remember a few realities about two-year-olds, specifically:

- They don't know how to share
- They have trouble understanding time
- They will say no

Two-year-olds might share a toy—momentarily. Then they will want it right back. On the whole, two-year-olds can't share. They might share at times, but they won't do it intentionally. They might offer someone a toy, but that doesn't mean they'll be happy when the other child takes it.

Understanding that two-year-olds in general can't share will help you approach any situation—play dates, sibling interaction, visits with family—with the proper parameters in mind. Bring some of your child's toys, but don't be surprised when he can't share, and when he cries, whines, or argues about sharing a toy (or having to compete for your attention), instead find a way either to distract him or to change his focus. This is far more effective than urging, "C'mon, let's share."

Your two-year-old will share in time, but expecting sharing behavior this year is not completely realistic. You might as well be speaking Urdu to your child. Two-year-olds don't know what a *minute* is and haven't yet familiarized themselves with the common phrases of our culture. They only understand one unit of time: *now*.

This doesn't mean your two-year-old isn't going to learn how to wait. He will. It's just that he doesn't know how to wait right now, so once again: distract and refocus him. When you need a moment to yourself, keep him busily occupied.

Two-year-olds hear *No!* and *Don't!* all the time, so they say it all the time. If you can, find a million ways to say *No* without saying so directly. Say: "I'm glad you're drawing, but let's use the crayons on the paper, not on the floor. The floor isn't for drawing." Or, "I know you don't want to share the blocks, but we can't throw them at our friends. That hurts."

It is important to note that yes, this is tiring. Sometimes you may feel silly explaining why throwing things, for example, is not good behavior. But such a strategy is more effective than constantly saying *No*. In the end will save you the aggravation of being told *No!* in turn by a two-year-old.

Chapter 5

Building Blocks
of Learning

When parents consider their two-year-old to be showing evidence of learning, they often refer to a moment of recognition—when a child sees her mother, for example, and utters the word *mama*. True learning consists of a complex process of making connections. When your child says *mama* for the first time, she is connecting an ability to speak with a desire to communicate with you. Connections occur in the brain when babies are exposed to information, are stimulated by their environment, and are engaged by others. Learning is dynamic and often spontaneous.

Early Learning

Between the ages of two and three, your child will start to form more abstract concepts about the objects and people she can identify. For example, she'll begin to connect the image of a horse she sees in a book with an actual horse she sees on a nearby farm. Even more, she'll begin to generalize that all horses make neighing sounds. As you might gather, a sophisticated process of conceptualization is underway in a two-year-old.

 Fact

Toddlers ask questions about what they see, taste, and touch. Your answers should be brief and simple, because two-year-olds can't process complex ideas. If your child asks, for example, why cars need gas, you can say that the gas makes cars move. A one- or two-sentence answer is enough.

Toddlers come to learn and understand by means of touching, tasting, and moving. Many two-year-olds still put foreign objects in their mouths (though by the end of this year, they'll know they shouldn't) and want to touch things directly rather than just observing them from behind your legs.

Exposure and Absorption

One of the marvels about a young brain is that it grows dynamically. As a result, a child forms connections and comes up with ideas that someone hasn't necessarily given her. A two-year-old's brain also grows with experience, which a child gathers by taking in information through his senses (tasting, touching, seeing, hearing, and smelling). This absorption takes time; it is a process that can't be rushed.

So when your child is sitting in the grocery cart and wants to hold the red pepper you're purchasing, let him. Let him touch it, smell it, and don't worry if he hits it against the cart. He is learning; he is not being disobedient or trying to mishandle the object.

In fact, talk to him about what he's doing, without drawing conclusions for him. Ask him specific questions: "How does it taste? Do you like how red it is?" Use as many words as you can and explain what you know about peppers, even though your child is not concerned about such details. "I love peppers in salad. Do you know that you can cook peppers or eat them raw?" This level of attention takes time, of course, but your approach will be rewarded when your child goes to school exhibiting an eagerness to learn more about the world.

Early Talents and Preferences

At the same time your two-year-old is learning more about the world, you are learning more about her. At this stage in her life she already demonstrates distinct preferences for activities and objects. She picks out favorite toys and enjoys, say, taking walks more than watching TV, or listening to music more than going swimming.

Although your child is too young for you to rule out activities she might become interested in later, you should certainly encourage her current interests as much as possible. If she likes to scribble, get her paper and crayons. See if there are art classes in your area for two-year-olds. If she likes books, take her to story time at a local bookstore or library. Such exploration of budding interests allows your child to see that learning can continue, enabling her to discover even more.

During this year you'll find your child becoming an expert in one or two subjects, such as trucks or dinosaurs. While it's often boring for a parent to hear endless recitation of the names of trucks or to have to read his child the same book over and over again, this repetitiveness is common to almost all children, so you should get used to it. It marks an early stage of learning as children begin to go into deeper study of a favorite topic.

Validation

There is another reason to encourage your child's inclinations: You are all the while validating who she is. At the age of two, your child's basic sense of self comes from the way you respond to her. So if she's enjoying an activity (kicking a ball, for example), the more positively you respond to her interest, the more likely she will stick with it. If you show no interest, her enthusiasm wanes. And if you discourage the activity, there's a good chance she will interpret this as personal criticism. In other words, she'll conclude, "Mommy thinks I'm not good at this."

Children need you to witness them. Even more, they need you to give them feedback—preferably loving and supportive feedback—about what you are seeing. At two, they trust your eyes and responses more than they trust their own.

Safe Exploration

Given two-year-olds' readiness to put new objects into their mouths and to smash new toys on the floor, you had better keep a close eye on them. The fact is, two-year-olds need to be watched as closely as younger babies. Even though they understand more than infants, they aren't more knowledge-able about their surroundings. Although actively learning, they haven't yet developed the ability to monitor themselves all the time.

 Essential

When you need to give your two-year-old important infor-mation—about safety, for instance—make sure you get down to eye level so that he's looking directly at you and then speak. If necessary, say, "I need you to look at me." This eye contact will give your words more impact.

The good news is that when you explain to your two-year-old why he can't do certain things, such as put small objects in his mouth or stick his fingers in light sockets, before too long he will understand you. Many parents have a *three-times* rule. They expect to have to point something out three times before their two-year-old actually hears and understands it.

This three-times rule holds true not only for two-year-olds but also for most people. Because it takes awhile for any of us to learn something new, try not to expect your child to hear and understand what you're saying the first time you say it.

One strategy is to try to teach your child a rule using more than words alone. Show him, if you can, the danger of what he's doing (not by hurting him, of course, but with a hands-on explanation). Try to demonstrate the right way to do something. Then finish by letting him try, if possible, the right way to do something.

The gas station; the grocery store; your kitchen; the homes of relatives; the park: These are all places your child finds fascinating and where he can learn much about the world. Exploring the world with your two-year-old is fun. (When was the last time you actually stopped to smell the roses?) But that means it also can be slow-going.

Not only do two-year-olds sometimes run when you don't want them to, they also stand still during times you want them to move. This can present a parenting challenge. Having a bit longer attention span than they used to, they will stop at something that interests them and not want to budge if you rush them. Nor are they as easily distracted as they used to be. Although their ability to focus is still undeveloped, two-year-olds are able to concentrate on one thing for ten minutes.

Encouraging a Love of Books

The value of encouraging your child to be curious about, to look at, and to enjoy books cannot be overstated. Acquiring the skill of reading is important for your child's self-development as well as to her success in life. Solid reading skills help a child learn and process information.

Two-year-olds are most engaged by books with large, colorful pictures or ones having thick and heavy pages they can turn, by short stories, and even by books consisting solely of words identifying what's on the page. They also like pop-up books and books with material glued on the page that they can touch.

Providing Variety

One way to encourage a love of books is to make adult books, newspapers, and magazines accessible to your child. At first he will try to tear the newspapers and magazines (and maybe the books), so you'll want to discourage that. At the same time, don't make the mistake of assuming he isn't old enough to enjoy books, magazines, and newspapers. This requires some foresight on your part. You can try giving him older newspapers and magazines that you don't mind being ripped, or you can make a no-ripping rule about reading material.

 Fact

Even though your two-year-old can't write, you can let her scribble with large crayons and encourage her to try writing her name. She will just produce scribbling, of course, but she might not know the difference between her scribbles and handwriting (most two-year-olds can't distinguish letters). But she will be proud of what she's written.

It is important not to make your two-year-old feel that books are off-limits. As your child approaches the age of three, you can use glue sticks and ripped-up magazines and newspapers to make collages. You can also make personal books for your child. Glue or tape photographs of people your two-year-old knows as well as things she likes onto construction paper or even onto the pages of a photo album (you can label the pictures). She can look at them when she's at day care or at bedtime.

Reading on a Regular Basis

Most likely you are already reading to your toddler before bed each night. You can also use reading as a way to soothe her when she's upset or to distract her when she's focused on wanting a toy. Reading is also a good activity when she's tired but doesn't want to sleep.

Make regular reading easier and more convenient by carrying small books in the diaper bag, buying waterproof books for the bath, and taking your child to bookstores and libraries for story times. One advantage in bringing your two-year-old to a bookstore or library is that even if she doesn't love books in general, she is likely to find a book on a topic that appeals to her, such as dinosaurs, ballet, or puppies.

Focus and Attention Span

The attention span of a two-year-old is variable and is very much subject to his moods. Although less easily distracted than he was at one, he will generally spend only a minute or two looking at any one thing.

At the same time, sometimes your child will become fascinated with an object and be unable to let go of it, both literally and figuratively. If it's small enough, such as a little toy, he will want to hold onto it and maybe sleep with it. If it's safe for him to do this, let him. If not, together find a safe place for him to leave the toy overnight.

 Essential

It's easy for a two-year-old's room to become over-crowded with toys. This can prohibit him from fully exploring particular toys. It sometimes helps young children to be presented with fewer choices. Rotate toys in and out of your child's playroom. That way he won't become overstimulated by the sight of so many different toys at once, and when the other toys reappear, they will be new again.

Some two-year-olds actually hoard toys because they aren't sure these will always be around. The concept of *object permanence* refers to a developing understanding that objects will indeed stay around. Although children learn this basic concept when they are very young, they aren't always certain of its reality.

You'll notice that the degree of self-centeredness in a two-year-old can actually extend to not wanting other children, even a friend, to play with one's toys. When a child's dislike of sharing is combined with the uncertainty as to whether an out-of-sight object remains around, you can understand why sometimes he might react very strongly when he can't have something he wants. You'll need to work through this seeming irrationality with your two-year-old, rather than chastising him for being unable to share and let go of his toys.

Counting

Toddlers understand just a few mathematical concepts—notably, one, two, and lots or more. They can't really distinguish between very small numbers. Although two-year-olds might pronounce numbers from one to ten (and are likely to do this by the time they turn three), they don't connect the words with actual amounts.

Teaching Counting Skills

Like the value of using long words regardless of whether your two-year-old understands, you should feel free to count items for her out loud, such as the food you get at the grocery store or toys you're playing with. Just don't expect her to be able to count along with you. Introducing her to basic arithmetic is helpful and will give her another way of understanding the world around her.

Reading numbers on a page is difficult for children because, as with letters combined to form words, they represent something abstract. So when you are teaching your two-year-old how to count, hold your fingers up or line up toys so she can connect the numbers with their meaning.

Time and Money

At two, children enjoy playing with pretend money, clocks, and watches because they are mimicking your behavior, even if doing so makes no real sense to them. Like letting them wash dishes or play with dolls, this imaginative play is beneficial, enabling them to familiarize themselves with adult notions and concerns. You can cut money up out of green construction paper and give your two-year-old one of your old wallets. Then let her shop in the house and pretend to buy her toys.

If your child is interested in a clock, show her how to wind it and how the alarm goes off at a certain time. Many children like stopwatches, too, because they can click them on and off. Remember, concepts of time and money do not really start to make sense to a child until she is around five. Nonetheless, your two-year-old listens to what you have to say about money and time even if she does not understand their meanings.

Choosing a Preschool

In many community school systems, children are eligible to attend preschool starting at two years and nine months years old. And if your child has been in day care as a two-year-old, he may graduate into a different program within that setting. Preschool programs for children approximately thirty months old should focus on social and emotional development rather than on intellectual ability. This doesn't mean that the games and projects your two-year-old participates in don't promote learning, but the emphasis should be on fun and social interaction, not on achievement.

Even without a hard-core educational focus, however, attending preschool has been shown to be advantageous for all types of children, especially those from challenging or underprivileged environments. Head Start programs, for example, expose children to reading, books, numbers, art, and science in ways that might not otherwise be available at an early age.

There is no question that children benefit from preschool. Working together in groups, being separated from parents for short amounts of time, and learning the rules and manners of school help children do better later in school. Most children attend preschool from just before they turn three until they are five, at which time they start kindergarten. Having two years of early schooling improves their reading and math scores later.

 Fact

Preschool programs range from day care that includes school-like elements to two- or three-day weekly sessions that meet only for two hours a day. Some programs that meet in churches, temples, or mosques stress religious training; others are owned by national chains (such as Bright Horizons) with set curriculums for children of specific age groups.

Is Your Two-Year-Old Ready?

Although preschool benefits all children, you still need to determine what type of program—characterized by its length, teaching style, and environment—is right for *your* two-year-old. Some children thrive in the structure of preschool. They like being active for most of the day and enjoy the social stimulation of other children. They also bond easily with adults other than parents and family members. These children might do best in an all-day program with a schedule.

Other two-year-olds, of course, find the prospect of preschool intimidating and aren't yet ready for a formalized structure. They might enjoy schools with less structure, in which free time to play and to participate in smaller groups are the norm.

There is no one right way to direct preschool. Although there are certain skills two-year-olds should be developing (such as drawing a straight line or acquiring a vocabulary of a few hundred words), your child no doubt will master these with or without a formal teacher.

What to Look For

No matter what type of program you decide is right for your two-year-old, there are some prerequisites every pre-school should meet. First, the TV should rarely—if ever—be on. If you see a television in a preschool classroom, and the teacher tells you the class watches TV or a movie every day, walk out the door. This isn't teaching, it's babysitting—and not even good babysitting. TVs are not beneficial in any way to young children.

Second, the school should be spotless. Certainly you'll want to see pictures hanging on the wall. The room should look comfortable and not be intimidating to a two-year-old. In addition, it should smell clean; the bathroom and food areas should be very clean. Look at the floors to make sure there isn't dirt on them. Look at the outside play area. It should also be safe and clean.

Third, ask the director of the school to explain the school's focus and daily schedule. If she can't answer those questions with clear, easy-to-understand answers, that should be a red flag. Ask her about expectations for two-year-olds. Do her expectations seem realistic? Also, be sure to inquire about discipline methods. The teachers should never use physical force or withhold food or positive attention. Find out if the school has ever had to ask a child to leave its program. Being unable to handle typical developmental issues should also be a red flag.

Finally, bring your child to the school and make note of her impressions. Does she seem comfortable? Does she seem intrigued by the toys and the various play areas? Your child's input is as important as any criterion when choosing a school.

Although educational background can't guarantee that an early-childhood teacher will be loving and kind, it can assure that a teacher will understand the typical behavior of a two-year-old. Most states offer licensing programs and short certifying programs for preschool teachers. Graduating from these programs should be a minimum requirement for your child's teachers. You should also make sure that the preschool is licensed and insured. All teachers should be CPR-certified, too.

Chapter 6

Play Time

There are two interrelated ways to look at the play-time of a two-year-old. First, you might consider such activity to be work, in the sense that play is the work of a two-year-old. As two-year-olds spend their day playing, play functions as an opportunity for learning. The second way of understanding play is as a kind of freedom from work. That is, sometimes a person, especially a two-year-old, shouldn't have to work. If children happen to learn while they play, that is secondary because the real point of play is to have fun.

Friendships

Although at two your child has friends and favorite companions, his friendships do not look like your friendships or even the way they will look in just a year or two. Currently his friendships center around children who want to play with the same toys (often at the same time). Two-year-olds understand that some children play with dolls, some with blocks, and some with balls. They like the children who play with the toys they like.

Two-year-old children know that some people are boys and some girls, using superficial clues (hair length, clothes) to figure out who is which. At this age many boys' and girls' favorite toys often divide along stereotypical gender lines. When you arrange play dates between your child and children of the opposite sex, however, they typically do not mind being together.

From the age of two to three, your child's friendships revolve around one or two children he sees in day care or with you. In other words, his friendships are based on physical proximity and time spent together. These experiences of finding activities to do together and of trying to share help your child get used to the basics of friendship.

Many two-year-olds like to play with an older child, whom they often idolize and mimic. Usually this is a good way of learning habits and behaviors that will help them play with others as they get older. But they can't help learning some negative behaviors, too (from the older child, that is). In this case, just remember that your two-year-old isn't distinguishing between what's acceptable and what's not; he's just acting like the big kid.

Short Play Dates

Play dates consist of a number of variables, such as amount of time spent together, number of children involved, and whether all the parents stay or just drop their children off, returning in an hour or more. The key to a good play date is communicating with other parents.

 Question

My son has trouble when children come to our house, but he behaves well in others' homes. Why?
He may have trouble sharing his own toys or even sharing you. Some children are territorial and just become bothered by having other children in their space. Reassure your child that the other children are only visiting, his toys still belong to him, you are still his parent, and you love him the most.

For two-year-olds, a play date is often best kept short. An hour or two is ideal; this allows the visiting child to check out all the toys. Typically at first he will simply move from toy to toy, thrilled by all the new things to look at. Eventually he'll settle on something to play with. Don't worry if the children don't play together but instead stay near each other while playing separately. This is entirely age-appropriate.

Some important rules govern play dates. First, always ask the other parent if the visiting child has any allergies. The child may want to bring his favorite blanket or toy from his house to feel more comfortable. Second, since naps are part of the daily routine for children at this age, ask the parent if the time period you are suggesting works for his child's nap schedule.

Third, if a parent is dropping off a child at your house, be sure you have her phone or cell phone number. Fourth, always make sure you have some healthy snacks on hand, since two-year-olds can get hungry at any time.

Long Play Dates

There may be times when you find yourself caring for another two-year-old for a few hours or even for an entire day. This actually shouldn't be considered a play date, insofar as you have to be responsible for a lot more than playing. Assuming that you will have to feed the other child and help her settle down for a nap, find out her complete daytime schedule. And consult the other parent ahead of time about whether watching some TV or a movie is allowed.

Some parents find a long play date easier if the children will be going out of the house and there will be lots of activities in which to participate. The fact that moving from playing in the house to playing in the park to going back to the house for lunch would exhaust a toddler is usually viewed as a plus.

Safe Toys

The minimum requirement for any of your two-year-old's toys is that they be safe. These days most toys are tested and must pass federal safety guidelines. Under the Child Safety Protection Act (CSPA) and Consumer Product Safety Commission guidelines, toys for children under three should have soft, rounded edges, simple construction, and bright primary colors. Toys that contain small parts or that can break into small pieces are banned for this age group. Furthermore, be especially careful with any small ball or toy that contains a small ball; these must meet a size safety test and include an explicit choke-hazard warning.

 Essential

Water toys can become water-clogged and breed germs. Shake out all water toys after a bath and leave them in a dry spot rather than in a wet pile. If you can't get water out of a toy, pour vinegar inside the toy and flood it with water to disinfect it. Don't use chemical cleansers on toys.

Product recalls are issued for many toys, but even if a product is not recalled, it's possible that children are able to break it in a way that renders it unsafe. Always help your two-year-old clean up so you can check his toys to be sure they're still safe to play with.

Toy Size

When your child in a store is begging you for a toy car or a doll with removable clothes, you might be faced with the *under three* issue. You've probably noticed that a lot of toys are labeled *not safe for children under three*. You, of course, have a child who is approaching age three, which means either you can follow this rule to the letter or abide by it more loosely as the year goes on. The decision depends on your child. Some children learn very early on not to put things in their mouths while others are compelled to taste everything, even when they are past the age of three. If your child fits the latter profile, you should follow the *not safe for children under three* rule strictly, even extending it past your child's third birthday, if necessary.

If your child does put toys in her mouth, you also need to make sure that the toys you buy, if at all possible, aren't painted or made with other chemicals. Since wood toys can splinter, be sure these have been properly sanded and made with nontoxic chemicals.

Durability

Large plastic tricycles, plastic playground toys, and plastic play kitchens—sometimes it seems as if plastic toys will never die. They last forever, and you hate to think of them rotting in landfills. Despite the fact that plastic doesn't disintegrate, you'll notice that it does rip and parts break off.

There are ways, though, to make sure the toys you buy last and remain safe for your two-year-old. First, teach your child how to take care of his toys. Every play session, however many children are present, should end with clean-up time. Your two-year-old is capable of picking up toys and putting them away where they belong.

Washing and dusting toys makes them last longer and stay in safe condition. You can use all-natural orange cleaner (which is nontoxic) on most toys and apply water with a little dish soap on plastic toys.

Fun Activities

It's tempting to take your two-year-old to all sorts of cultural events, museums, and public places, now that she is able to walk on her own as well as be awake for longer periods of time. You need to remember, though, that children at this age are quite determined to explore places and things on their own terms. While you may want to see the whole museum, realize that your child may only want to play in the toddler play area.

Understand also that your two-year-old is not yet ready to sit quietly or stand still for long periods. An hour at the museum is probably her limit unless she's tired and ready to sit in a stroller (after having had a chance to run around and explore).

 Fact

Look to cultural institutions in your community for age-appropriate programs. These are often inexpensive and allow adult access as well. Such programs often involve art projects, playing instruments, or listening to storytellers, all of which are ways for your two-year-old to get used to listening, following directions, and working with others.

If you're going on an outing with your two-year-old, be sure you're prepared. Consider keeping a stocked diaper bag in the car in case you end up being somewhere longer than you expected. Also be sure you have snacks and drinks on hand for your child, since not all museums and libraries can accommodate the food choices of young children. Always bring some toys to keep your child occupied (if you're lucky) while you're out in the world.

Everyday Activities

Even if you've been bringing your child to the same park or beach (or backyard) every day for two years, she will find something new and exciting to explore now that she's able to run, hop, and touch things she was previously unable to reach.

During this year your child will become more able to interact with you on shopping trips. So if you're at the grocery store, for example, you can ask her to get items for you or to hold things while you shop. If you offer her responsibility and engage her, she is less likely to have to look for ways to entertain herself.

Just as it is unnecessary to buy expensive educational toys for your child, it is also unnecessary to pay for expensive experiences. Parks, some museums, libraries, bookstores, a friend's house and backyard, the beach, a hiking trail, a nearby nature preserve, or any local attraction are good places to bring your child without spending a lot of money.

Life is fun for a child this age because she understands more of what she's seeing and doing. She'll want to share more with you and, even if you can't understand exactly what she's saying, she'll be conveying what she's seen and what she's been doing. It's very important that you listen and make eye contact when she's talking so that she understands that her opinions and experiences are valuable and meaningful.

Playing with Water

Toddlers love water. In fact, on rainy days you should be well prepared to go outside with rain boots, umbrellas, rain coats, and hats. Don't let bad weather stop you from exploring the world. In the first place, a toddler stuck inside on a rainy day may get antsy without a lot of space to run around in. Second, the experience of seeing the world when it's wet will thrill your two-year-old. She will jump in puddles, splash, and pick up slippery rocks and sticks.

 Essential

If your toddler is cranky, try putting her in the bath. It's not so much that water will magically transform her mood, but being able to play in water just might do the trick. Give her pots, pans, and spoons and let her play with them in there. She'll be happy as a clam.

Another great way to play with water is to get out the hose, if it's warm enough outside, and let your two-year-old help you water the garden or wash the car. Two-year-olds are always happy to have a grown-up responsibility and even though your child's participation may slow down your work, you will delight her with the opportunity to help you.

Other water-based play ideas: Bring cups and plastic pitchers outside for your child to fill with the hose. Or let her stand in the kitchen and use the sprayer at the sink (she'll make a mess, but she'll love it). Get some water paints and let her play with them outside. Whatever the water play, always be conscious of water safety.

Playing with Mom and Dad's Things

Although your child has her own toys, no doubt she walks into your bedroom and wants to play with your shoes, take the clothes out of your dresser, or find out what's in your closet. If you work on a computer, she will want to try it. If you have a workbench, she will want to try your tools; if you cook, she will want to make something with you.

If it's not dangerous, find a time when you can use your tools and equipment as toys. This isn't always possible, of course, but keep in mind that your child is paying you a high compliment. He isn't trying to ruin your things. It's just that he doesn't quite yet understand (although you can start teaching him) that some things are toys while others must be treated more carefully. He is simply trying to play the way he sees you playing.

Pots, Pans, and Boxes

Pots and pans, along with boxes, are perhaps the most creative and fun toys a child this age can have. Add a wooden spoon and she'll bang, stir, pretend to make dinner and serve you, and build with these objects. Give her a set of her own pots and pans, some Tupperware bowls and wooden spoons, as well as other cooking utensils (as long as they aren't sharp), and she will be endlessly engaged.

If you've gotten a package recently, hand the box to your child. It can be a bed for her doll, a hiding place for his stuffed animal, or a special place for her to keep her collection of princess jewelry. Boxes can be blocks, houses, furniture, hiding places, theaters, and obstacle courses.

To use boxes even more imaginatively, you might want to have lots of masking tape on hand as well as scissors (which only you can use), magic markers, crayons, glue, and art supplies. Boxes make wonderful canvases.

 Fact

Being able to cut well, trace, paint, and transform a box into a car or a house will turn you into your child's hero. Young children are amazed by the talents their parents display, so take every opportunity you can to make things for your child. This will inspire and impress her.

Two-year-olds often need help with inspiration for projects, unlike older children who can immediately find ways to turn a box into a rocket ship or a boat. Be aware that your two-year-old will need your help with these projects, which they will very much enjoy making with you.

Arts and Crafts

Two-year-olds are in the process of developing their fine-motor skills, which means they are learning to use their fingers in a much more exact way than previously. Handing them toddler scissors and other art supplies gives them opportunities to practice these skills. Understand that at this age, they can only hold large paint brushes, large crayons, and other big art tools.

One handy art tool for a two-year-old is glue or paste since this allows them to use their fingers to make something. You can put glue and paste on an amazing number of materials, including wood, cotton balls, feathers, string, blocks, glitter, and, of course, paper. You should also keep toilet paper and paper towel rolls (which can become horns, telescopes, and binoculars), as well as fabric scraps and old clothes (they can be doll clothes and stuffed animal outfits).

Activities that allow easy cleanup are imperative when you're the parent of a two-year-old, enabling your child to help you get the job done as well as make sure you don't get aggravated after you've been playing. Two useful things to have on hand: plastic-coated tablecloths, which you can put on the floor or over a table to catch spills, and hand-me-downs from older children or just old clothes that your child can ruin.

Scribbling

Your two-year-old's art will not be representational (that is, pictures of things and people) but will consist mostly of scribbles, the result of simply playing with crayons, pencils, and markers to see what they can do. Although your child's drawing skills are still rudimentary, she will this year become able to draw a circle. It won't be perfect, but it will be round! Although you may not be able to recognize what your child draws, keep in mind that you do not need to communicate that to her. Simply say, "Can you tell me about this?" rather than asking, "What is this?" That way she won't know you can't tell what she has drawn.

Painting

If your child is going to paint at home, you might try doing this activity outside so that spills and drips will just fall on the ground. Or you can work in the basement or garage.

Here are two great painting projects for children.

- Drape a nonfitted bedsheet over a clothesline and let children paint the fabric with permanent paint. You now have a new tablecloth!
- Have your two-year-old dip sponges and cookie cutters into paint, then press them onto paper or fabric.

Painting is good for two-year-olds because even though it requires fine motor skills, they can use very large brushes. Keep in mind that a painting work surface should be bigger than one used just for work with pencils and markers. You can use large sheets of butcher-block paper or newsprint as a canvas for large projects.

Blocks and Building

At the same time your child is exploring what the large muscles of his body can do by running and jumping, he is also trying out his small muscles by practicing motor activities with his fingers. In fact, some of the skills his pediatrician or teacher possibly looks for is whether he is able to build a tower of blocks, or to thread blockholes with a shoestring, as well as engage in nonplay activities such as dressing himself. These demonstrate a level of physical development he has only recently attained.

 Essential

Some toys and activities that encourage fine-motor development are Legos, sewing kits, and toys that require putting shapes into sorters. Musical instruments also develop fine-motor ability as do activities that require physical manipulation, such as moving blocks along a wire or using a magnet to draw a ball along a course.

Your two-year-old also enjoys using his fingers to help you around the house. So give him jobs that allow him to hold and carry objects he previously hasn't been able to handle. He can roll up socks and put them in a drawer, sort silverware in a drawer, and stack books into a pile.

Physical Play

Two year-olds love to use their bodies in interesting new ways. They enjoy pulling and piling as well as jumping and hopping. You'll notice also that your two-year-old likes to push things, so toys that roll will entrance him.

Most children this age like large trucks and cars that they can use their whole bodies to roll and move across the floor, in the sandbox, or the backyard. Your child is also able to jump with both feet and walk on his tiptoes. You can play *follow me* types of games with him at this age. Ask him to do what you do, then run, jump, walk funny, or slide and he'll enjoy mimicking you.

He will also enjoy dancing, so rather than turn on the TV, put on a CD and get the both of you moving. Children this age love to play with their favorite music in the background. They break from playing to sing and dance. Your child may not realize that he needs to move his feet and will instead just wiggle around. Or he'll jump and hop but not really listen to the music. Whatever he does, encourage him and make sure you're moving with him.

At this age, your child will be able to use his feet and legs to push himself forward on pretend bikes, which are large wheeled toys that don't require a lot of balance or speed. This is wonderful exercise for his legs that will also give him a sense of freedom and accomplishment.

 **Alert!**

> If you're going to the market or taking a short trip out of the house, don't be so quick to bring along the stroller or bother taking it out of the car. Instead, let your child walk more often now as well as climb stairs while holding the banister, if he can reach it.

Your two-year-old will want to balance on benches and try to scramble up rocks. In fact, often his eyes are more adventurous than his body! Take your child on walks in the woods and near water so he can practice walking on uneven surfaces as well as feel comfortable in the outdoors. Remember, though, that if you walk into the woods, don't go so far that your child can't walk back out on his own—he's now getting heavy and you don't want to have to carry him back!

Chapter 7

Toilet Training

M any parents wait eagerly for the day when they can say goodbye to the hassle and expense of diapers. Others fear the toilet-training process and worry about their child feeling stressed during this period. The most important point about toilet training is not to rush the process and instead to stay calm. Keep in mind that this period is not a competition—whether your two-year-old is potty-trained now or later, he will learn eventually. The more naturally you let your child get used to using the bathroom, the easier it will be.

Toilet Training Readiness

When your child is still an infant, he has no awareness of when he urinates or has a bowel movement. As he becomes a little older, he might notice only that he feels uncomfortable when his diaper gets too wet or dirty. A toddler, on the other hand, suddenly becomes aware of the physical sensation of urinating and having bowel movements. He might instinctively squat or stand still to pay closer attention to the feeling. He may smile with the release of urine or, if he's having a bowel movement, he might begin trying to control its passing, grimacing with the effort.

Your two-year-old's face and body will be your first clues that he has become aware of his body doing something. He is not ready to use a toilet at this point, but you should begin to talk to him about what is happening. Make your comments nonjudgmental, informative, and validating by saying something like, "You're peeing. That's great!"

 Essential

As with his learning to stand and to walk, you can't really train your child to use a toilet. He will progress naturally through the multiple stages of bathroom readiness. Your job is to help him get used to what his body is telling him and praise him as he learns each step of the process.

This phase of awareness most likely lasts a few months, often between the ages of eighteen months and thirty months, although it varies greatly from child to child. Such growing awareness has no correlation with your child's mental and emotional development. Some children are more in touch with their bodies than others. Some children are so absorbed in playing and in exploring the world that they barely pay attention to their bodies.

Your Attitude

What you say and the way you say it can help your child make a connection between what his body is doing and the necessary steps for keeping clean, comfortable, and healthy.

If you make diaper changing boring and matter-of-fact (no books or toys), your two-year-old will be less likely to want to hold onto this activity. The major trap parents fall into is in paying too much attention to their child's not using the toilet instead of providing their child with the motivation to start using it. There is no such thing as mechanically training your child to use the toilet. Rather, toilet training consists of a physical readiness on your child's part coupled with your ability to help him navigate this phase.

The Signs

Eventually your child's awareness of his bodily functions comes not just after the fact but while he is urinating or having a bowel movement. As time goes on he will realize what is about to happen to him before it does. First he will make a connection between feeling the physical urge, on the one hand, and the actual experience of urinating or having a bowel movement, on the other. With time he will connect this advance bodily sensation with what he actively needs to do—get to the potty and remove his clothes and then properly relieve himself.

A child not only has to be psychologically ready to use the bathroom, but he also has to have an element of control over his body. For instance, he needs to be able to control his bladder in order to wait until he gets to the toilet to empty it. Like other learned processes, this ability requires both psychological readiness and physical development. So even though a child might practice holding his bladder, he can't be made to do this if his body isn't physically able to do so.

Your two-year-old, then, has a good deal to learn in terms of bodily awareness and self-control before he is able to use the toilet or potty. So it's important to look for several signs, not just one or two, before you decide whether your child is ready to start learning to use the bathroom.

An indication that your toddler is ready to give up diapers will take the form of communication with you. He now wants you to change his diaper soon after it's been soiled. Or he will try to control his body, waiting until he can go somewhere to privately take care of business. (Children still using diapers have been known to go under tables or to hide away in closets.)

Other signs from your child include:

- an interest in the bathroom, going into it or sitting on the toilet
- telling you what he is doing ("I'm peeing!")
- his diaper is dry after a nap
- having one or two predictable bowel movements a day

It is actually easier to hold in a full bowel than a full bladder. Consequently, many children control their bowel movements before their urine output. You may notice your child looking around for privacy before he has a bowel movement. Or if you're in a restaurant or around friends, perhaps he waits until he's alone with you. When you notice this ability to wait and control his body, you can try teaching him to use a potty or the bathroom.

The Potty

Before using a toilet, many children nowadays first use a potty, which is a low toilet seat that parents put on the floor. The opening is smaller so that a child doesn't feel like he could fall in (as children sometimes feel on a toilet). Some potties come with removable tops that can be put on top of a real toilet seat. That way a child can sit on the toilet without feeling like he might fall in.

Potties need to be cleaned. Some come with plastic liners, but others need to be wiped or rinsed out each time they are used. Because they sit on the floor, they get dirtier just by their location.

Some children want to use a toilet rather than a potty because they don't like sitting so close to the floor. Or they find the potty dirty, since their waste isn't flushed away quickly. Other children adore the potty and drag it from room to room, even sitting on it in front of the TV. You won't know which type of child you have if you don't have a potty in your house. So you need to buy one (or more if you have more than one bathroom or story in your house) and keep it accessible.

Pay attention to your child discover what his natural response to it is.

 **Alert!**

There are pros and cons regarding potties. If your child requires a potty, you may need to carry it around with you. If your child prefers the toilet, you will have to use whatever one is available. Stay nearby while he's on it since he may not be able to get on and off by himself and could also fall in.

In terms of your child's training, it doesn't matter whether he prefers the toilet or the potty. Eventually your child will use a toilet. What matters is that your child use whichever feels easier and less stressful.

Toilet Training Methods

There is no one successful way when it comes to teaching your child how to use the bathroom. Each child feels comfortable learning in her own way. It a skill that does require some teaching, however, because a child needs to learn how to remove her clothes, to sit down (or stand, in the case of a boy) and wait, as well as how to clean herself afterward.

Many of these steps, particularly clothing removal and wiping, are actually impossible for a child to do on her own at this age, so she will need your help with these for a few months. Cleanliness needs to be so important to you that you don't leave it to your two-year-old to wipe herself. Just because she's ready to use a potty or toilet does not mean she's able to clean her body. Be matter of fact about wiping her. As with helping your child learn any necessary skill, it is important that you are supportive, making sure to follow her lead.

The Reward System

Offering a reward is a popular way to encourage a child to use the potty or toilet. Each time your child sits on the potty or toilet, you give her a sticker or an M&M (only one, since you don't want to be overfeeding candy to your child). If you do use the reward system, be careful not to reward actual peeing or pooping, but, rather, reward your two-year-old's effort. Also, you don't want to give preference to one bodily function over the other. Each effort at the toilet earns the same reward. Get your child wholly involved in the process by letting her pick out the stickers she wants and then putting them in a place of her choosing.

In other words, you want your child to feel like she's rewarding herself for learning how to use the potty or toilet, rather than you rewarding her for accomplishing something. The idea is that you are supportive of your two-year-old just for trying. The risk of this system is that your child learns how to get a reward by showing effort but is not motivated to go beyond effort.

The Weekend Method

The weekend method works best when a child is clearly ready to use the bathroom without needing much encouragement. To try this, set aside a weekend (you might choose a three-day weekend or, if you're a stay-at-home parent, a series of days) when you can focus on her not wearing a diaper. You will need to be able to take her to the bathroom whenever she needs to go.

 Essential

False alarms are inevitable in toilet training. When children feel the slightest sensation in the lower half of their bodies, they often think they need to "go." Follow every request to accompany your two-year-old to the bathroom because it will take her some time to distinguish the sensations of needing to pee or poop from other feelings, such as having gas.

If possible, take your two-year-old to different bathrooms in the house so she doesn't associate only one bathroom with using the toilet or potty. If it seems she enjoys your chasing her around to get her to the bathroom, then this method is not working. It should not be turned into a game.

If you do try the weekend method, you have to get your child on board by telling her in advance that she'll be saying goodbye to her diaper on a certain day (at least during the daytime). Explain to her that you'll stay home for a day or two so you can help her use the bathroom.

Every few minutes you're going to have to ask your child if she needs to use the bathroom, so that she pays attention to how she's feeling. Once she starts playing or getting engrossed in an activity, she's likely to forget she's not wearing her diaper. False alarms are just as likely as accidents, although it's possible that, if the timing is right, your child will take to the bathroom with little or no confusion.

Using Pull-Ups

Pull-ups are diapers that a child can pull up and down. They are like underpants but are easier to clean up if a toddler has an accident because they are disposable. Some children love pull-ups because they give them reassurance that they won't soil themselves and wherever they are sitting. Then they can get to the bathroom to take care of business.

 Fact

The earliest that Western children start to toilet train is at about thirty months. At this age, they know enough words to be able to communicate if a toilet training method isn't working for them. So listening to your child's opinions and respecting her feelings during this new stage in her life is especially important.

On the other hand, some children don't like pull-ups—or even understand their use—because they feel too much like diapers. Pull-ups, like the potty, will either work for your child or not. You'll just have to try them out and listen to your child's feedback.

Resistance to Toilet Training

According to the father of psychoanalysis, Sigmund Freud—
and to countless psychologists, psychiatrists, and therapists
following him—toilet training is not just about developing the
ability to use the toilet. As has been noted, it is also about self-
control. And, even more, it becomes bound up with parental
approval for a child, particularly if he has an accident. There
is also the possibility your child may fear that with his increasing independence you will no longer take care of him the way
you used to.

With so much riding on a child's use of the toilet, not all
children are thrilled to let go of their diapers. In fact, some
children actually resist it. Many children experience fear of
failure, fear of losing your approval, and fear of change.

Questions about toilet training are some of the most
stressful a parent can get, especially when they come from
relatives, all of whom seem to have an opinion about when
and how a child should be "trained." Although it might
be difficult, you need to make this issue a private matter
between you and your child. Not making the pressure you
feel become pressure your child feels is a way of respecting
her boundaries.

If your child resists this new stage, the first thing you should
do is befriend her. Just as you would do with any friend, try to
understand how she feels and offer her your love and acceptance. Just receiving such support from you might give her
enough security to let go of her fear.

Responding to Your Child

As with other child development issues, such as temper tantrums, biting, or crying, the best thing you can do is to remain dispassionate and offer your support. In other words, don't turn the bathroom into a power struggle. Insisting that your child learn something or accomplish something she may not be ready for will not help her learn the skill sooner. On the contrary, such pressure may make her unhappy and stressed.

Your role in this situation is to offer encouragement and instruction at the same time that you let go of control. It is your child's body, after all. She needs to understand that her body belongs to her and to no one else. This autonomy is important to a child's sense of well-being and self-esteem, so let your ego take a back seat to hers. Most children will want to start using the toilet or a potty when they are ready. Ultimately, they are the ones in control, so if you are making toilet training a parenting ego trip, you may get very frustrated.

Working Through Your Child's Fear

Even though your child may not be able to explain the nature of her fears or worries, you can still talk to her about them. Reassure her that it takes everyone time to learn new things and that you love her no matter what. She will learn eventually; all children do.

See if you can determine what precisely is bothering her. You might check-out from the library some books on toilet training. Or you can frame the discussion in terms of *other children* who are worried about attaining this new skill.

(Remember, your child is only two, so she won't catch on to your indirect approach.)

Keep in mind during this process that many children do not begin to use the bathroom until they are well into the age of three. Sometimes their timing is a matter of physical development, other times it's a function of emotional development. Regardless, you need to understand that when exactly your two-year-old toilet trains has nothing to do with her intelligence or capability. It is just one skill she has yet to learn in her very young life and signifies nothing about developing skills in other areas.

Handling Accidents

Even after diapers are no longer needed, you need to keep in mind that accidents do happen, especially to two-year-olds. It is imperative you understand that accidents in no way indicate that your child is doing something wrong. Your explanation of accidents as being a natural part of the learning process will help your child feel confident and secure.

Accidents are most likely to happen when your child is engaged in another activity, such as playing, and simply doesn't *hear* her body saying that it's time to go to the bathroom. She is still getting used to noticing the signals her body gives her, as well as learning to interpret what these mean.

You need to pay attention to your two-year-old for clues about when she might need a bathroom. Often, boys will put their hands on their gentitals, and children of both sexes will wiggle or hop. Remind your child that she needs to use the bathroom and that if she delays (because she's having fun), at a certain point she will go whether she's near a toilet or not. Accidents can be good teachers, serving as reminders to your child of what can happen if she holds in her bladder or bowel movements too long.

Regression

After a child has been consistently dry for a few months, it is surprising when, as sometimes happens, he starts consistently having accidents. This might happen at night and even during the day. You might be able to connect this regression with a recent event in your two-year-old's life, such as the birth of a new sibling or moving to a new house. When children feel stressed, confused, or worried, they may forget their recently acquired abilities. They don't do this on purpose. In fact, such a relapse may bother a child as much as whatever is worrying him in the first place.

 Alert!

Regression is not typically conscious. Many of the skills your two-year-old acquires at this age require physical (rather than cognitive) development, so when a new task comes along, it takes a little while to adjust. If the regression lasts more than a few days, take your child to the doctor to make sure he doesn't have a urinary tract infection.

In reassuring your child that he needn't be embarrassed about his accidents, let him know that this behavior is natural for young children. Tell your child that most two-year-olds aren't even toilet-trained yet, so he shouldn't be upset with himself. Then think about whether anything is going on in your family that could be bothering him. If you know what the trigger is—a new baby, a new home, or some other event in your lives—offer him support and love.

It may seem overly sensitive to consider that small children can become so upset by changes in their lives. Certainly for generations many parents assumed their children just rolled with the punches. They understood their children's accidents as a sign of misbehavior rather than a possible indicator of confusion or distress. These days, however, parents and physicians take a more respectful approach toward the trials and tribulations of growing up. Children want to please their parents and meet expectations that are realistic. To help them, parents need to give their child love and support. This allows children to honestly handle their feelings, including accepting whatever stage of development they have currently reached.

Preparing for Being Away from the House

One reason some parents don't look forward to toilet training their children is because they know they will have to use public restrooms (even ones they would normally avoid), since small children cannot wait as long as adults can.

If you are a parent who doesn't relish the idea of relying on public restrooms, there are a few things you can do to cut down on the likelihood of having to use, say, a gas station toilet. First, make sure your child goes to the bathroom before you leave home. Second, if you're out in a place that you think might have clean bathrooms, take your child to use the toilet there rather than relying on her to tell you when she needs to use it. You might also bring along pull-ups if the car ride is extra long and she doesn't always stay dry when she sleeps. That way, if she falls asleep she'll be more comfortable and you won't have to wake her up.

If you know you're going to be in the car or away from the house for a while, you might also consider bringing the potty seat (with liners) along with you. This way, a clean toilet is always close by. Bring wipes, too, so you can clean your hands and the seat if your child soils it.

As the parent in charge, you need not only to expect accidents to happen but to be prepared for them. Clean underwear for your two-year-old, an extra outfit, and wipes should go with you everywhere until your child is at least three. Keep these in the car just in case.

Toilet Training in Day Care

If your child is in day care or attends some type of preschool, the teachers will typically have experience (as well as opinions) of how they can best help him use the bathroom. The teachers will have practice in dealing with toilet training with other children. Sometimes, in fact, as a result of seeing their friends and classmates using the bathroom at school, children are motivated to try out the school toilet even before the one at home.

To find out whether your two-year-old is experimenting with the potty or toilet (which at some facilities are smaller and lower to the ground for small children) at school or in day care, you may need to raise this issue with a staff member. A teacher or a day care provider should have a good understanding of how ready your child is to give up diapers.

 Fact

Schools sometimes discourage early toilet training (with children under three) because younger children are more likely to have accidents and to regress. Most schools these days do not expect children to be trained until they are at least two years and nine months of age, although children are more often between three and three and a half.

Extra Support

Children are loved and cared for not only by their parents. Teachers, grandparents, babysitters, other adults as well as older children are sometimes called upon to teach young children the ropes. This is a good thing and can help take the pressure off a toddler, helping him see that everyone eventually learns how to use a bathroom. Having other caregivers involved also takes the pressure off the parent, and with less pressure may come more successful efforts on the part of your two-year-old.

On the other hand, toilet training is one of those topics on which many people have opinions, and not all of these are helpful. If a grandparent or teacher isn't handling the situation the way you would like her to, explain what you're doing and offer exact instructions on what you need her to do. Remember that, just as with children, it may take the adults in your life a little while to adapt to your instructions. Since they probably have your child's best interests at heart, explain why you are asking them to follow your way (after acknowledging them for their help).

If you find your toddler is interested in the bathroom or if you're trying to start toilet training, be sure to let the other people closely involved in her life know. They will be able to encourage her and might have some words of wisdom that you haven't thought of.

Let Your Child Lead

One day your child may want to wear underpants, the next day he wants his diaper. One day he sits on the potty, the next he decides he hates it. Toilet training is a big step for a child—diapers not only provide a real source of comfort and security, they offer an opportunity for the adults he loves to take care of him. In addition to grappling with physical changes at age two, your child will have mixed feelings about not being a baby anymore. So let his moods hover over the situation without putting too much emphasis on any one state of mind. Eventually he'll work through his ambivalence and be a preschooler who uses the bathroom reliably.

Bed-Wetting

Children's nighttime bladder control develops at a different rate than that for daytime control. In fact, many children continue to wear pull-ups at night because they sleep so deeply that they don't wake up when they urinate. Nighttime control may come even years after daytime control. Many young grade schoolers still wet at night. This problem tends to run in families.

 Essential

Nighttime bowel control is usually reached before daytime bladder control. If your child soils her bed at night, you should probably talk to your doctor; she may have a stomach bug or other digestive problem that prevents her from going to the bathroom at regular intervals.

If your child is a deep sleeper, you can try limiting her liquids in the evening as well as waking her in the middle of the night to get her used to going to the bathroom at night. You can also just let her wear pull-ups at night until she no longer needs to. Usually nighttime bed-wetting, especially with children under the age of five or six, is not a sign of any problem. If, however, you suspect that your child is worried or not sleeping well and peeing during the night on top of this, you can talk to her about it. At this age, chances are this indicates a lack of physical development and is nothing to worry about.

The more relaxed you are about toilet training, the easier this stage is for your child. If you find yourself in a power struggle over this issue, you'd do well to back off altogether: no reminders with your two-year-old; no bribes; no mandatory potty times. Make diaper changing routine and let yourself relax about the whole issue. Sometimes such an approach turns the tide, allowing your child to choose the toilet on her own terms.

Chapter 8

Toddler Nutrition

Your two-year-old's health is closely tied to how much he eats, what he eats, and how active he is. Obesity and weight-related diseases affect about 20 percent of all children today. These problems include diabetes, asthma, bone disorders, and other health problems. It is very rare for weight-related problems to be genetic in origin. Overweight children are almost always overweight because of lifestyle—and very young children have only the lifestyles that their parents or other caregivers create for them.

Healthy Choices

Creating a healthy life for your two-year-old is a matter of making choices that encourage physical activity and a diet of nutritious foods, as well as fostering his cognitive and emotional development. Many parents don't realize that what a child eats for breakfast, for example, can affect his energy level and mood throughout the day. Moreover, studies have shown that children who eat a healthy breakfast do better in school. And even if your two-year-old isn't going to preschool, he is busy learning all day long. If he's hungry or tired because he hasn't eaten healthy food, that in turn affects how he thrives during early childhood.

Making healthy choices may seem like a lot of effort, but there are two additional rewards other than experiencing your child's good health. First, if you focus on promoting a healthy life, chances are you will live more healthfully too. In fact, many parents have found their own eating and exercise habits changing as a result of caring for their child's well-being. The second reward is that healthy foods are less expensive than highly processed treats, and healthy children need less medical care. It saves money to live a healthy life.

Nutrients

Children need a balanced diet, which means eating a proper amount and variety of nutritious food. The nutrients people require contain a combination of protein, carbohydrates, and fats. At a basic level, protein builds muscle and tissue, carbohydrates provide the body with energy, and fats not only provide long-lasting energy but protect various body parts and help the brain to function properly. Children need all of these essential nutrients and never should be put on diets that mimic the eating fads of adults.

 Fact

> A balanced diet includes a variety of food types, such as meats, fish, poultry, vegetables, fruits, and whole grains. It is less important to worry about nutrients than to be sure you are offering your two-year-old all types of food. Even if he just takes a bite or even refuses it, at least you've given him the opportunity to try something.

Children need balanced diets not just for protein, carbohydrates, and fats but to be assured of eating a range of vitamins and minerals, both of which play a pivotal role in helping the body to function and grow properly.

Whole Foods

One of the most effective ways to ensure that your child is eating nutritiously is to give him whole foods, which are unprocessed foods. These are foods without chemicals, extra fats and sugars, and other unhealthy ingredients. Try substituting the following whole foods for popular processed foods in your two-year-old's diet:

Processed Food	Whole Food Replacement
Fruit roll-ups	Apples, strawberries, bananas
French fries	Baked or mashed potatoes

Processed Food	Whole Food Replacement
Chicken Nuggets	Baked chicken breast
White bread	Whole-wheat bread
Chips	Carrot sticks, sliced vegetables

The whole foods listed above are not only more nutritious, having more vitamins, minerals, and fiber, but they have fewer calories.

Milk and Juice

With the recent increase in overweight and obese children, experts have pointed a finger at whole-fat milk and juice as culprits. In moderation, however, both milk and fruit juice have a place in a healthy eating plan.

Milk is an excellent source of calcium, protein, complex carbohydrates, as well as of vitamins A, D, and B_{12}. Two-year-olds should drink whole-fat milk because the fat in milk is a good source of calories and energy. Fat is also good for nerve development. From the age of three on, children can drink lower-fat milk.

 Essential

Reading nutrition labels is a must for healthy eating. Two ingredients you should always stay away from are high-fructose corn syrup and partially hydrogenated oils. These chemically altered substances have been linked to weight gain. Having no nutritional value, their presence is an easy way to determine if a food is unhealthy.

Juice is a slightly different matter. There are two types of juice: the type without added sweeteners and the type that is really just a lot of sugar with some fruit juice and water added. To distinguish between the two kinds, examine the nutrition label. If it lists "high-fructose corn syrup" or "added sugars," then it's a juice to stay away from.

Fresh orange juice and cranberry juice sweetened with other juices rather than sugar are the healthiest juice varieties. Apple juice and white grape juice have little nutritional value and are also high in calories. Healthy juices contain antioxidants that fight free radicals—chemicals that age the body. They also contain vitamins and sometimes added minerals, such as calcium.

Juice becomes a problem when consumed in large amounts. Eight ounces of juice a day (comparable to one adult glass) is not a caloric problem, but more than that means taking in a lot of calories without additional nutritive value. Your child should drink plenty of water. If she likes juice, you can always cut the juice with water to reduce the calories she's drinking. If your child comes to depend on the sweetness of juice, as many two-year-olds do, offer her milk or water sometimes. Milk is much better than juice as far as supplying nutrition.

Plenty of readily available foods are full of added sugar, which increases their calorie count without adding nutrients. Spaghetti sauces, canned soups, and frozen and boxed entrées often have added sugars and preservatives (chemicals such as MSG) that add flavor but can also make a food needlessly fattening. After all, fresh spaghetti sauce consists simply of tomatoes, olive oil, and spices. A lot of added sugar isn't necessary.

If possible, always choose the least-processed foods in creating meals for your two-year-old (and the rest of your family). Your addition of oil, butter, and flavorings will not add nearly the fat and calories as does a manufacturer's heavy hand.

Junk Food

Junk food is food that, though edible, is devoid of nutritional value. Some snacks may start as natural foods but after processing—which replaces the fiber and all of the nutrients with fat, sugar, and chemicals—they barely resemble their original form in nutritional content.

Most fried and packaged foods are full of ingredients that don't add any nutritional value. Even foods made with all-natural ingredients like homemade cakes and cookies can be considered *junk.* insofar as they are very high in calories (especially in calories supplied by fat and sugar) and contain few nutrients.

Why You Should Avoid It

Junk food includes almost any food that has a lot of calories but little nutritional value. A two-year-old needs only about 1,000 to 1,400 calories a day, depending on how active he is. That does not add up to much food. For example, a handful of Cheerios, a glass of milk, and a piece of American cheese is about 200 calories. Include an apple and half a hamburger and you've added another 350 calories. Finally, a glass of juice, a cup of macaroni and cheese, some green beans, and yogurt will raise the total to about 900 calories.

The calories in junk food are a problem for two reasons. If your child watches an hour of Sesame Street and eats four cookies, she's consuming about 280 calories but only burning one-seventh of that. Those 280 calories are devoid of any vitamins, minerals, fiber, or protein. The carbohydrates are *simple*, which means that if they aren't burned quickly, they turn to fat. Finally, because they lack nutrients, they don't really satisfy your child (even though they fill her belly). In other words, she still wants to eat more because her body is in search of nutritious food—so she eats more junk until something healthy comes her way.

Why Junk Food Sells

If you look at much of the food packaged for children (pushed through commercials and advertising), you'll notice it features gimmicks that appeal to small children (candy "dinosaur eggs" in oatmeal, cereal containing marshmallow treasures). Even though your two-year-old may be enticed by the playful features of junk food, you fortunately have complete control over what you buy and what she eats. Simply buy the healthier versions of these foods.

Fast Food

Many parents, especially those with more than one child plus an outside job, find themselves in the car when mealtime rolls around. It's difficult to resist the lure of McDonald's and other fast-food chains when you're hungry, your child is hungry, and you're pressed for time.

Fast-food restaurants present both advantages and disadvantages. Most places do offer a selection of healthful foods. In recent years children have more nutritious options to choose from, such as spring water or juice instead of soft drinks, apple slices instead of French fries. Unfortunately, high-fat, highly processed foods are still readily available, so you have to train yourself to make conscious decisions at the drive-through window. You can be sure that if you're eating French fries, drinking soda, and eating a large burger, your two-year-old will want that meal, too.

Family Restaurants

When looking for places to eat with their children, parents often try to stay away from fast-food restaurants, alternatively turning to chain family restaurants, assuming they will find more healthful food. The reality is that many of the dishes available in these types of restaurants are not much better, in terms of nutritional value, than fast food. Menu options for children are similar to those of fast-food restaurants: macaroni and cheese; chicken nuggets; grilled cheese; hamburgers with fries. All of these foods have one thing in common: high fat content.

Although it's fine for your two-year-old to eat these prepared foods once in a while, it is much better to frequent restaurants that offer a full range of healthful selections. These consist of vegetable side dishes, fresh fruits, broiled and baked meat, poultry, and fish, and other nonfried options. You usually stand a better chance of ordering nutritious, fresh food at locally owned restaurants and diners rather than at chain restaurants.

 Fact

Children's meals in family restaurants are appropriate portion sizes—for adults, that is. Even if your two-year-old does not eat all of her meal, that's usually because it is the size of a healthy adult meal to begin with. So don't force her to eat all of it.

Eating at Home

Studies have shown that the healthiest eaters, both children and adults, are those who have a majority of their meals at home. There are several reasons for this.

In preparing foods at home, you can control the amount of fats and sugar in meals. Also you are able to cook a meal that is well-balanced, combining vegetables, fruits, whole grains, lean meats, poultry, fish, and dairy products. And at home you have control over portion sizes (which is important as your two-year-old gets older).

Natural Eating

"Be sure to clean your plate." For generations, children were taught to eat all that they were served, rather than eating just enough to satisfy their appetites. This acquired propensity to overeat leaves us feeling we need more food than we actually do, with the result that we've come to expect extra-large portions.

As primary caregivers, parents have an innate desire to feed and nourish their children, but sometimes, regrettably, this takes the form of prodding their child to overeat. It's difficult for parents to give a child control over his own appetite. For when your child is little, you believe you know what's best for him. In reality, though, your two-year-old must be allowed to listen to his own stomach, just as he has to become attuned to when he needs to use the bathroom.

That doesn't mean your child should serve himself. It is still up to you to provide him with healthy food and to discourage any less-than-nutritious choices. Your task is simply to encourage your two-year-old to eat as much nutrient-rich food as he needs—no more, no less.

Almost all children are born with a natural sense of how much they need to eat. If you respect this self-regulating function of the body, you will allow your child to gauge his own food requirements for staying healthy.

If your two-year-old is hungry again an hour after eating, offer him more healthy food rather than an unhealthy treat. Again let him eat until he is full. Just consider all of his eating times, whether meals or snacks, as opportunities for nutritious consumption. Many adults create a dichotomy between meals (healthy) and snacks (treats), but such behavior should not be extended to your child. With a two-year-old who is learning to eat properly, you need to make sure that even his snacks are healthy.

To support this goal of always eating wisely, use language that teaches your child to listen to his body. "Have you had enough?" "Are you still hungry?" "Do you need more?" Even two-year-olds, when asked, can answer these questions. This questioning routine is far more helpful to your child than your telling him how much to eat.

The Dangers of Dieting

One factor shown to lead to adult weight gain, ironically enough, is childhood dieting. Food restriction can turn a child into someone who is always hungry, leaving her never able to learn what "full" feels like. This can burden a child with an excessive psychological need for satisfaction from food. Should you begin to worry excessively about the weight of your two-year-old to the extent that you restrict her food intake, she may never learn to eat properly.

As has been noted, only a very small number of children are overweight due to genetic factors. Children's body weights are distributed across a range on the standard growth chart, which means that some two-year-olds are naturally heavier than others, but the majority still stay within the normal range.

Rather than trying to stop your child from eating too much, offer her normal *child-sized* portions of healthy foods. Once she's eaten a proper meal, feel free to offer her a normal child-size portion of dessert, such as fruit and a cookie, a small dish of ice cream, or a small slice of cake. Keeping sweets away from your child will only make her want them more. Instead teach her how to enjoy food in moderation.

There are numerous ways adults diet in order to lose weight. They limit how much food they eat, they cut out entire food groups, they binge and then starve themselves or, worse, they purge. Very few adults eat properly, whether in terms of nutrition, amount of food, or eating habits.

 Alert!

Parents often pass their own bad eating habits along to their children. Even small children have been known to worry about weight when they hear parents discussing their own weight concerns. Watch your language and prejudices about weight around your two-year-old, for your goal is to raise someone who feels comfortable with her body and is attuned to its signals.

Passing these eating patterns down to your child is as dangerous to her health and well-being as passing down your smoking or drinking habit. No matter what your age, dieting does not foster a good relationship with food, does not help you lose weight intelligently, nor does it allow you to feel healthy in the long-term.

If you're a mom or dad who struggles with issues of weight, or your relationship with food and exercise, first consider the strain this places on yourself. Then work to help your child develop a healthier relationship to food, exercise, and weight management. Encourage her to listen to her own body when it comes to food, respect her need to eat until she's full (and no more), and give her every opportunity to be active.

Physical Activity

One of the major reasons so many children struggle with their weight has to do with a lack of activity. Children just don't run, jump, and play as much as they used to. They watch TV, use computers (even at the age of two), and are driven everywhere instead of walking. This sedentary lifestyle is as bad for children's health as it is for adults.

It isn't always easy to build activity into your day—or even into your two-year-old's routine. Many parents have to drive to health clubs, and classes (such as swimming, Gymboree, and yoga) are expensive.

The best way to get exercise is simply to build activity into your daily life and into the routine of your two-year-old. If you have to run errands, drive to a central place, park, and walk through town. After dinner take a walk as a family. On Saturdays and Sundays make plans that involve activity.

Promoting an active life is not just important for keeping your child's weight down. Active children have better moods, sleep better, do better in school as they get older, and retain their good health (assuming they remain active) into adulthood. It is up to parents to create active lives for their two-year-olds.

Turning Off the TV

A direct connection has been made between the amount of TV a child watches and his weight. This potential danger might seem insignificant to you when your two-year-old can't turn on the TV on his own, but it is not. Because if the TV is on in your house, even if tuned to adult shows, there is a good chance your child will be watching too much TV before too long. And that increases the likelihood he'll be eating too much while he's watching, not to mention watching inappropriate shows.

Getting Outside

When you plan your child's day, you can promote healthy and safe activity by including time outside as much as possible at parks, playgrounds, and in your neighborhood. Unless it's raining very heavily or is extremely cold or hot, your two-year-old will enjoy being outside. Just be sure to use sunscreen and clothing that is appropriate for the weather.

Toddlers love to explore the outdoors. Yours will typically do one of two things: He will move very slowly as he studies the bugs under the rocks, the rocks along the sidewalk, and each flower in every yard. Or he will run as fast as he can.

 Essential

If you're bringing your child outside to play, take a ball, a kite, or other outdoor toys for her to play with. Even though she won't be able to play with them exactly as they're supposed to be used, she'll enjoy using them and trying them out.

In any case, let your child investigate the outdoors in his own way (assuming he isn't running into the street). You shouldn't be worrying about your two-year-old burning calories or getting strong; just make sure he's spending his time actively rather than sitting too much.

Inside Games

You can also be active inside your home. Your two-year-old is likely to run around in the house if you let him, of course, but you can also help him to be physically active in a more constructive way. Sit on the floor and roll a ball back and forth between you, or get a large exercise ball and help him balance on it. You can play "Follow the Leader" and have him mimic you as you jump, walk backward, and hop. He may not be able to do all of these things, but after watching you he'll try!

Chapter 9

Feeding Your Two-Year-Old

Toddlers' eating habits are a study in contrasts. On the one hand, it seems as if they never stop eating. On the other, it's common that just when you sit them down to have a meal, they manage only a few bites. Despite such patterns, children continue to grow and even thrive. The fact is, their stomachs are small, so they can only eat small amounts of food at a time. Small meals throughout the day typically are best for two-year-olds.

Parenting Style and Childhood Weight

In June of 2006, the journal *Pediatrics* published a Boston University study by Kyung Rhee, M.D., which found that the more rigid a parent was about food, the more likely that parent was to have an overweight child. The researchers followed 872 children and assessed their parents' parenting style. They also concluded that young children who received parental love with clear-cut boundaries were less likely to be overweight by the time they started school.

Parents walk a delicate line between setting boundaries and supporting their child's individual needs and personality. Previous eras often considered a child to be a blank slate that parents (and society) needed to mold and instruct in order to create a good person. During the 1960s, some parents rebelled against this attitude, believing instead that children left to their own devices would grow up healthier and happier. Without being negligent, these parents let their children have more control over their own lives.

Indulgent Parenting

Permissive parents provide their children with neither daily routines nor set boundaries. For example, a child with permissive parents often doesn't have a set bedtime or a routine that makes for restful sleep. His meals aren't provided at set times or based on good nutrition. Permissive parents give their children too much freedom and then are often surprised when their children don't follow rules or know how to behave in a social situation. Permissive parenting does not, as these parents might hope, create strong children who can take care of themselves; rather, it makes children worry that no one is taking care of their needs. Consequently, they never learn self-discipline and good behavior.

Permissive Parenting and Eating

For most American children, high-sugar and high-fat foods, such as candy, chips, fruit snacks, and soda, are available all the time. When parents combine the easy availability of junk foods with a permissiveness that, say, lets their children over-indulge their sweet tooths, the result is often childhood weight and health problems.

 Fact

> The Centers for Disease Control and Prevention estimates that 17 percent of American children ages two to seven-teen were overweight in 2003–2004 and the number is rising. This is not to suggest that parenting style is the only cause or predictor of a child's weight. Factors such as family eating patterns and cultural background also have been shown to greatly influence weight.

If you find it difficult to set boundaries for your child, remember two things: First, children feel better and they do better when they have an adult setting limits for their behavior. Permissive parents often think they are making their child happy by giving him what he *wants*, but in fact you will make your child happier in the long run if you give him what he *needs*.

Second, if you are already permissive, in order to parent more responsibly you don't have to go to the opposite extreme and become *authoritarian*. You simply need to set some boundaries between you and your child. Establish routines and be sure she knows who is in charge of the situation. Let her know that you set the rules, but—an important caveat—you create those rules based on what's best for her. This is known as an *authoritative* (not to be confused with an *authoritarian*) parenting style.

Authoritative Parenting

It turns out that the most successful parenting style, in terms of raising happy and independent children with high self-esteem, is *authoritative*. Authoritative parents are strong parents, which is not to say they are harsh and rigid; the contrary is true. They set rules for their child but they are at the same time open and responsive to changes in her schedule, to her needs, and to the way she learns.

These effective parents—for they are those with the happiest and most successful children—strive for a balance between control and empathy. Studies show that such parents produce children who are secure, independent, and have a high degree of self-control. They clearly serve as the boss and teacher of their child, but always by way of giving her respect, empathy, and some role in the decisions that affect her.

In other words, as an authoritative parent you are in charge, but at the same time you give your child some latitude. You choose your battles. For example, when your child gets dressed in the morning, you might give her some options by asking if she wants to wear her green shirt or her striped shirt. If she wants to have waffles or have candy for dinner, you might tell her that dinner has to be fish, rice, and vegetables, but she may have some candy after she eats a proper meal. This way your child has input, but you are in control.

Children of authoritative parents feel safe because they don't have more responsibility than they can handle. Also, because they are listened to and treated with respect, they feel confident in their ability to make good decisions. An authoritative upbringing is associated with social competence and lower levels of problem behavior in both boys and girls throughout adolescence and into early adulthood.

Authoritarian Parenting

Authoritarian parents, the antithesis of *permissive* parents, believe that they should be in control of their children and that there is only one right way to do things—their way. Children of authoritarian parents often feel frightened and learn neither self-reliance nor self-control. They are more likely to rebel later in life. When it comes to food, children of authoritarian parents are more than four times more likely to be overweight than children of authoritative parents.

According to researchers, you are authoritarian if you expect your young child to sit or play quietly while adults are talking. (Remember, considerate behavior is something you want to *teach* your young child, not something you *expect* from him.) How often do you expect your child to go to bed without a hassle? Do you expect your child to be on his best behavior in public and to go to bed with no fuss? Authoritarian parents have unrealistic expectations of their child.

Even though such parents have very high expectations for their children's behavior, they don't provide them with the support they need or with the proper guidance. Consequently, children under an authoritarian parenting style have been shown to have weak social skills, low self-esteem, and high levels of depression.

Dietary Guidelines

No matter what your parenting style is, you likely know that children, like adults, need to eat from each of the food groups: breads and cereals; fruits; fats; vegetables; meat or other protein sources, such as tofu or legumes; and dairy. If they are offered all types of foods, they are more likely to get the nutrients they need as well as the proper number of calories.

An important factor to consider when preparing food for a two-year-old is that a child at this age has unsophisticated tastebuds. Although the rare child will eat the same creatively prepared foods his parents eat, most children like simple and recognizable foods.

Some great nutritious and popular foods for two-year-olds are:

- hard-boiled eggs
- yogurt
- bananas
- apples

- oranges
- carrot sticks
- chicken breast
- whole-wheat noodles
- whole-wheat bread
- strawberries
- green beans
- zucchini
- brown rice
- potatoes
- beets
- apricots
- cottage cheese

Most small children prefer foods that aren't mixed together and that are without complicated sauces. While a little salt and olive oil can add flavor, heavy sauces add unneeded calories and fat to your child's diet. Two-year-olds also tend to like the sweeter fruits and vegetables and to dislike anything that's bitter or sour.

Low-Fat Diets

Aware that fat consumption is linked to obesity and contributes to heart disease and other illnesses, parents these days often worry about their children's fat intake as much as their own. Although children are not prone to heart disease, parents have come to believe that cutting fat out of a child's diet early on will protect him from illness later in life.

 **Alert!**

The fats you should restrict in your child's diet are those that are added to foods. These fats, such as lard or margarine, are typically solid at room temperature and contain partially hydrogenated oil, a chemically altered oil. Having little nutritional value, they have been shown to be more likely to increase body fat than do natural fats.

The truth is, your child's body needs fat. The fat he eats, however, should be natural and, hopefully, of the omega-3 variety, as opposed to fat added to food (in the form of margarine and partially hydrogenated fat), omega-6 fats, and saturated fat.

Healthy fats are found in meats and poultry as well as in eggs, fish, oils, dairy foods, and nuts. Children under the age of five can eat whole-fat dairy foods because these contain the type of fat that helps the brain develop properly.

Low-Sugar Diets

An apple contains sugar, as does a lollipop. You might be surprised to learn that ketchup, bottled tomato sauces, and many other packaged foods also contain sugar. Natural sugars like those found in fruits are good for the body, however, providing energy and helping to keep energy levels high throughout the day. Added sugars, contained in candies, cookies, cakes, and other processed foods, are by comparison less healthy, contributing to mood swings, poor health, and weight gain.

Fat and sugar are often found in combination in unhealthy foods. Candy, cakes, and cookies, for example, are high in both. If you limit the amount of added sugar in your two-year-old's diet, you will go a long way toward limiting the amount of unhealthy fat he eats. That will help to keep his weight down and his health intact.

Processed Foods

Manufacturers do a lot these days to turn healthy and low-calorie food grown in nature into unhealthy, fattening, and non-nutritious versions. These processed foods are unhealthy, especially compared with the originals. A baked potato is a wonderful source of fiber, potassium, and carbohydrates. Add a little sour cream, and you've got some protein and calcium. Turn that baked potato into French fries, and you've lost the fiber along with other nutrients and increased the saturated (unhealthy) fats. Feed your two-year-old foods in their natural state as often as possible.

Toddler Serving Sizes

Appetite, which is associated with growth and energy levels, regulates the amounts people want to eat. Because children grow at a slower rate from the age of two on, their appetites shrink a bit.

One reason parents become frustrated with their child's eating habits is because they often serve their two-year-old servings similar to what they give the rest of the family. They often forget that even though their two-year-old is eating grown-up foods rather than baby food, he is still not much bigger than he was a year before.

Most packaged foods are sold in sizes that are far larger than what children (and, for that matter, adults) should eat. So don't be surprised if your two-year-old eats only a few bites of whatever you give him. He isn't necessarily being stubborn, he may just be listening to his body.

A toddler's stomach is the size of his two fists put together, so when he's left alone himself to eat until he's full, he will most likely eat only a cup of food (at most) at any one time. As a parent it's important you keep your child's stomach size in mind, because encouraging your two-year-old to eat past his point of fullness is not good for his body. Nor does it help him to develop good eating habits.

There are a number of foods that your child shouldn't eat at two, or that at least need to be served in a specific way until he's a little older:

- **Nuts**. Nuts are a choking hazard because they are small and don't dissolve or break easily. Keep nuts away from your child until he is at least four.
- **Whole grapes**. Grapes are a terrific snack but another food that can easily choke your child. If you do feed them to your two-year-old, cut them in half.
- **Meat**. Children often find beef and chicken hard to chew and swallow. Cut these foods into very small pieces or serve them in the form of cold cuts (e.g., sliced turkey and chicken), which are easier for your two-year-old to handle. Do stay away from highly processed lunch meats.

- **Popcorn**. Popcorn is dangerous for your two-year-old because pieces can get lodged in his throat.

You should also be careful serving any snack food your child may be tempted to take too much of, such as chips or pretzels. Your two-year-old might put too many of these in his mouth and then be unable to chew them. Teach your child to take small bites and to eat slowly.

Dealing with a Picky Eater

Perhaps you have faced the following dinnertime quandary: You're in the mood for a sirloin steak and mashed potatoes, but your fussy two-year-old wants only macaroni and cheese. What do you do? Ideally you find a way to make meals that please everyone. To keep everyone happy, it's helpful to keep some rules in mind.

- **Children like simple foods**. If you want to serve a steak dinner with potatoes and vegetables, keep the sauces and heavy spices off your two-year-old's servings.
- **If you find something your two-year-old likes, stick with it.** For example, if he loves cheese, feel free to include it in most meals, which might encourage him to eat other foods (like cheese on vegetables or cheese on whole-grain bread).
- **Think outside the box**. If your child loves oatmeal, give it to him for dinner every once in a while. Breakfast foods are great dinners for small children.

- **Your two-year-old won't starve as a result of pickiness.** She might not eat dinner or she might eat only a few bites, but eventually she will eat.

These are generalizations, of course. Some children (even two-year-olds) love all kinds of adult foods and never develop a taste for packaged foods. If that sounds like your child, consider yourself lucky.

Even holding realistic expectations about the way your toddler eats—small portions and more frequent meals and snacks—you may still have a poor eater on your hands. Perhaps your two-year-old eats only one food, doesn't eat enough, or eats only sugary foods. If you have a troublesome eater on your hands, first be careful not to turn the issue into a power struggle between the two of you. To avoid such a situation, offer her all the foods you'd like her to eat without commenting on the importance of eating one over the other or telling her how much she should eat.

 Essential

A child only uses food as a bargaining chip if she can tell that that works. In other words, if you make your daughter's eating an issue, she'll know this is an area that gives her some power. So sometimes it pays to ignore your child's behavior.

Then, if she's still not eating, try to determine whether you have unrealistic expectations. Look at her two fists together and compare their size to the amount of food she's eaten. Is it really that much less? Or perhaps she's not eating for a reason. Two common reasons that children don't eat are illness or a behavioral issue. Ask yourself: Is she sick? Do the foods you prepare simply not appeal to her, or is she trying to use food as a means of controlling a situation?

There are times when your two-year-old refuses to eat and you have to determine how to handle the matter. Should you let her get up from the table? Should you make her a different dish? How can you tell what's really going on?

You should always offer your two-year-old the same food you've made for yourself or for the rest of the family, keeping in mind that she won't eat as much. First, let her sit without you commenting on what she's choosing or not choosing to eat. Then see what happens after the meal. Does she expect dessert? Later, does she eat a snack that isn't as healthy as the meal was? If so, you might well conclude that she's trying to eat only food she likes and to avoid the healthy foods you're serving her.

On the other hand, if she's not substituting snacks, the likelihood is that she's either sick or doesn't need to eat as much as you think. If she seems healthy and energetic, the latter is probably the case.

Two-year-olds can take a long time at the table, picking at their food or even ignoring it for a span of time. As much as you want your child to eat quickly, try to let her eat in relative peace. At two, she won't really be able to sit still for long or necessarily be engaged in the dinner-table conversation.

Food Strikes

But what if your child has figured out how to work the food system? What if she doesn't eat the healthy fruits and vegetables and instead asks for snack foods like chips or cookies? What if she is only hungry when meals are over? Even a two-year-old can get used to eating only sweet and fatty foods rather than the healthy ones you try to give her.

If you and your two-year-old have become stuck in an unhealthy food routine, you need to take a few steps to change the dynamic. First, you should take away the unhealthy food options. This is going to be tough, but just tell your daughter you've run out of the unhealthy item she is asking for. Then offer her something healthier to eat, even if it's snack time and not dinnertime. If your child is used to eating chips, for example, offer her whole-wheat bread with peanut butter or a slice of cheese. Once she realizes she's not going to get treats, she is more likely to eat with the rest of the family.

Vitamins

Because children can be such fussy eaters, parents often turn to children's vitamins to make up for missing nutrients in their diets. There's nothing wrong with this. Children's vitamins are formulated especially for small bodies and contain nutrients small children need, including ones they often don't get enough of (such as calcium).

One child multivitamin a day is plenty for your two-year-old, so don't think that just because this is good for her, she should have more. Some doctors suggest you supplement your child's diet with Ensure or other vitamin-enriched drinks. If you do so, these should be in place of, not in addition to, a multivitamin chewable pill.

 Alert!

> Children can overdose on adult amounts of vitamins and minerals, especially iron, which can be toxic to a young child. Do not give your two-year-old adult vitamins. Also do not let her eat too many fortified foods, such as cereals or power bars.

Sippy Cups

At two, your child can easily hold a small cup, especially one with two handles (as many children's cups have). But these days most parents give their children sippy cups, which don't spill when tipped over.

Sippy cups are practical because they are neat and don't require you to help your child drink. Still, they can make it very easy for a child to drink too much juice or milk. If possible, offer your child a sippy cup when you're in the car or when you don't want a spill. The rest of the time, offer her a regular child's cup.

There are other types of cups in addition to sippy cups that can help your child learn how to be responsible. For instance, there are two-handled cups that are easier for small children to carry. You can also find cups with flip-up lids that, though they'll spill if turned over, enable a two-year-old to drink from them more easily than do other cups. You can also get cups with attached straws, which children love.

What is important about cups is not the type of vessel but how much liquid it contains: Don't fill any cup too high. An inch of liquid in a cup for a two-year-old is fine at any given time. That way the cup is less likely to spill, and even if it does, not too much liquid will fall on the floor or on your child. Also, if you only serve an inch of liquid at a time, your two-year-old will be less likely to get too much in her mouth at any time.

Messy Eaters

When a parent spends the day watching a toddler, cooking for a family, taking care of the house, and perhaps working outside the home, it can be exasperating to watch a two-year-old sitting in his high chair or booster seat rubbing food on the table or throwing it on the floor. The situation is especially confusing when your child looks just adorable making a big mess and you don't want to discourage him from having fun. All the same, you want to encourage good manners as well as not have to clean the floor after every meal.

It's worth bearing in mind that two-year-olds are not being disobedient when they make a mess with their food. They are not intending to make a mess, in other words. Getting impatient with your child makes him feel that something is wrong with him rather than with what he is doing. In discouraging him from continuing to make a mess, you need to explain that the problem is with the mess, not with him. Say, "It's hard for me to have to clean up so much, so that's why it's important to keep food on your plate." Or, "Food is important because it gives you energy and helps you feel good, so try not to waste it by dropping it onto the floor." Even though these are obviously sophisticated notions to convey to a two-year-old, if you provide your child with this level of information often enough, eventually he will understand why his eating habits matter to you.

Potential Reasons for Messy Eating

One reason children make a mess with their food is because it's fun for them to see the effects of their physical actions. They might drop their spoon into mashed potatoes to see the indentation it makes or want to discover what happens to cereal if left in milk for a while. Even though your two-year-old has been eating solids for a long time, he has not lost his interest in playing.

 Essential

Two-year-olds don't eat that much at any one sitting, so offering your child too much food is almost inviting him to play with what he's not hungry for. Cutting down on his portions—and then giving him more if he asks—is one way to minimize mess.

There are a number of ways you can simultaneously allow your child to enjoy his mealtimes, teach him not to play with his food, and still keep your house somewhat neat.

You might try engaging your two-year-old in conversation during meals, so that he's entertained by you rather than his food. If after a while he isn't eating, just take his plate away and allow him to sit with you at the table (though he might only last a few minutes without something to play with).

Involving your child in food creation—stirring, layering cheese and turkey on a sandwich, decorating a pizza—is a great way to get him to try new foods. If he is allowed to play with food in a constructive way before the actual meal, he might be neater when it's time to actually eat as well as be focused on satisfying his whetted appetite.

Some dishes that children can help with include making pizza and creating cookie-cutter sandwiches. To make pizza together, buy a ready-made whole-wheat crust. Your two-year-old can help you roll out the dough. Once you put the sauce on, he can sprinkle on the cheese and choose other toppings. Small children often choose chicken rather than olives, mushrooms, or pepperoni for a topping. You can also make special pizzas with mascarpone cheese and fruit. You can find creative pizza recipes at *www.foodtv.com*. (Search under *pizza* in the recipe section.)

To make cookie-cutter sandwiches, choose the type of sandwiches in which the ingredients stick together, so the final product holds up. Peanut butter sandwiches, peanut butter and jelly sandwiches, cheese sandwiches, or cream cheese and jelly sandwiches work best. Then give your two-year-old some cookie cutters and let her cut shapes out of the sandwiches.

Fine Motor Control

Although there are those children for whom food functions as a play thing or art medium, it's more likely that your child has trouble eating neatly because he doesn't have enough fine motor control to handle his food properly.

There are a number of things you can do about this to make mealtimes a little neater. Letting your child eat with his fingers might help, because children who cannot yet control small muscles may have trouble holding a fork or spoon and getting it to their mouth. Another option is to cut your child's food into slightly larger than the usual bite-sized pieces so that he can easily pick them up. This only works, of course, if your child will be sure to chew his food well before swallowing.

Finally, give your two-year-old foods that are already somewhat neat. Keep the sauce on pasta to a minimum, for instance, and try to reduce the number of wet and squishy foods (such as mashed potatoes) your child eats. While messy eaters have fun with their food, they also want to feel they have mastery over their habits; they don't want their mealtimes to become struggles over manners any more than you do. Foods that are easier to eat also help your child feel more confident.

Chapter 10

General First Aid and Medical Issues

By the time your child is two you may actually feel like an expert in children's health. Between the shots, the well-baby checks, and the emergencies, you probably have the pediatrician's phone number programmed into your brain as well as cell phone. Chances are you've learned the difference between a cough caused by your child's inability to blow his nose and a see-the-doctor cough. Being a "nurse" is just one of the responsibilities that fall under the parent's job description.

First Visit to the Dentist

By the time your child is three, she should have visited the dentist at least once or twice. If your two-year-old has inherited unhealthy teeth and gums, however, she may already need to see a dentist more often.

 Fact

> Some dentists recommend that your child have a fluoride varnish, which cuts down on the incidence of cavities significantly. You can also give your child fluoridated water to drink (from plastic bottles) if your community does not have fluoride in its water. Too much fluoride has been shown to be problematic, so ask your dentist for recommendations.

Even though your two-year-old will lose her deciduous ("baby") teeth, these teeth play an important role in her overall health, affecting more than her dental health. Baby teeth are softer than adult teeth, so they need to be brushed as thoroughly and as regularly as adult teeth.

A dentist will check the health of your baby's teeth and gums for signs of decay. Infected or rotted baby teeth can cause problems later for the adult teeth, leading to stains, pits, and weak teeth and gums.

What to Expect

The dentist will take x-rays of your two-year-old's mouth (your child will wear a lead blanket to protect his body) to examine both your child's baby teeth and what's happening under his gums. He'll look closely at his teeth with instruments and a mirror. The hygienist will clean his teeth, and either the hygienist or dentist (or both) will talk to him about how to take care of his teeth. They may even ask to watch him brush.

Preparation for the Visit

Most children feel a natural distrust of the dentist and feel displeasure at the idea of visiting the dentist—they feel vulnerable having to sit still and keep their mouths open for someone who prods them with metal objects. To help your two-year-old get through this experience, be sure to describe to him in advance what will take place and what the office will be like. Explain that even though the dentist will be using metal tools, that they won't hurt him.

When you arrive at the dentist's office, introduce your two-year-old to the receptionist, hygienist, and dentist so that he feels more comfortable with them. They'll probably spend some time reiterating what they will be doing, and (if they're used to working with children) they'll let your child play safely with the equipment so that he isn't intimidated by it. And, of course, your child will probably go home with a new toothbrush!

It's a big deal for your child to go to the dentist, so congratulate him afterward for doing such a good job, and ask him how he felt about the visit. Talking about an experience afterward really helps children process what has just happened.

If the dentist finds any problems with your child's teeth, he'll point them out to you as well as recommend treatment. Likewise, if you have trouble brushing your two-year-old's teeth, you can ask the dentist for suggestions on better care.

Essential

Many dentists specialize in helping children feel comfortable during dentist visits. If you can, find a doctor who has made this a priority. Their offices can be less daunting and more fun than regular dentist offices, plus the dentist will know how to deal with a child who is scared or emotional.

If your child ever falls or gets hurt in the mouth—especially if she loses or cracks a tooth—see a dentist immediately. If possible, put the tooth or piece of tooth in a glass of milk (milk has nutrients the tooth's root cells need to stay healthy) and bring it with you. If it is nighttime, call the dentist and follow the instructions for an emergency that she's left on her voice mail or with the answering service. You may have to wait until morning to see the dentist, but it's possible the dentist or an assistant might be able to meet you and your child at the office after you describe the problem.

Vaccines

Two-year-olds have already received a number of shots, typically beginning in their first few days of life. Even so, at two they are more aware of what might happen at the doctor's office. In fact, your previously oblivious child may suddenly become afraid of going to the doctor's because he'll remember having gotten a shot there.

Recommendations for Vaccination

No matter how fearful your child is, of course, if he needs a scheduled vaccination, it's imperative you get it done. Immunizations protect children from a wide range of illnesses, many of which used to kill young children or irrevocably harm them. Typically your child will receive an inoculation series for DTP (fights diphtheria, tetanus, and pertussis [whooping cough]), polio, MMR (fights measles, mumps, and rubella), and Hib and PCV7 (pneumococcal) vaccines (both of which fight bacterial meningitis and some blood infections). Your doctor may also recommend a chicken pox vaccine and a flu shot.

Every state has its own schedule and regulations regarding vaccines, so you need to speak with your pediatrician about what your child needs throughout this year. You should have received paperwork and records of which shots your child has already had, because many of the inoculations are *booster* shots, which means they are part a series that is administered at specific ages.

Addressing Your Child's Fears

At two, your child may not anticipate having to get a shot, and chances are she won't ask you ahead of time whether she's going to get one. You should always tell your child in advance when you're taking her to the doctor, however. Even if you're sure she's going to be scared or nervous, you should not surprise her or trick her to get her there without a tantrum. Your child needs to know she can trust you and that you are honest with her no matter what.

 Alert!

If your child is sick, even if she just has a cold or bad allergies, reschedule the well-child visit and the shots. It's much safer and easier on your toddler to get vaccinations when she's feeling well than if she's contracted a virus.

Once you're at the doctor's office, your two-year-old most likely will be weighed and her height measured. Next the doctor will check out the rest of her body, typically saving the shots for last. If your toddler knows about the impending shots, however, she may spend the visit anticipating them, asking when they are going to happen. If she's very apprehensive or tense, it might be better for the doctor to give the shots sooner rather than later.

When the doctor or nurse brings out the needle (or needles, as the case may be), your child may suddenly get a look of panic in her eyes. Try to keep her focused on you and talk to her about something other than the needle. This is often very difficult; sometimes you just have to tough it out with her.

If your two-year-old gets hysterical, hold her torso and keep her looking at you while the nurse or doctor takes hold of the arm needed for the shot. Keep talking to your child in a soft voice, reassuring her that this will be over quickly. Don't yell or become emotional yourself. The good news is that this procedure really will be over quickly, and before the two of you know it, you'll be able to get your child dressed and out the door.

Staying Healthy

It's possible you think of good health as a gift over which you have little or no control, but in truth (chronic illnesses and disease aside) you can actively adopt many strategies to keep your child and yourself healthy. In fact, what works for one of you will work for the other. To assume that all you need do to ensure your child's health is simply relieve illnesses as they strike is insufficient. Prevention is the way to avoid having to subject your two-year-old to repeated cycles of antibiotics or other medications, most of which have side effects. Overuse of antibiotics is a concern of doctors because both children and adults can develop resistant bacteria.

The keys to good health for both your two-year-old and you include:

- eating well
- getting enough rest
- getting enough exercise and sunshine
- having a little stress in your life
- keeping clear of—and fighting off—germs as much as possible

It is impossible to germ-proof your child. Germs are everywhere, and being exposed to germs is part of life. As a matter of fact, exposure to different viruses and bacteria can actually strengthen a child's immune system.

The Importance of Cleanliness

There are a number of ways your two-year-old can pick up germs: from her diaper or in the bathroom, by touching toys or playing with children who are sick, or when out and about and near strangers who are sick and still contagious.

To diminish the risk of infection, wash your child's hands as often as possible and teach her to wash her hands. You may need to carry wipes with you when your child is this young because some of the places where she plays, such as the playground or the park, do not have convenient places to wash up.

 Fact

There is a difference between dirt and germs, as well as something that looks clean but is actually dirty. If someone has a cold and touches your child's face, he can get a cold. If your child plays in dirt, he most likely won't get sick. You want to protect your child from anyone who is sneezing, coughing, or sniffling.

Your two-year-old is too young to be expected to keep her germ-ridden fingers out of her eyes, ears, nose, and mouth, which are precisely where germs can enter her system. For this reason, it is very important to keep your child's hands clean.

Strengthening the Immune System

The immune system fights disease-producing organisms such as bacteria, viruses, fungi, and parasites. Just because your child is exposed to these organisms doesn't mean she will get sick. Some people have powerful natural defenses against disease, while others are more susceptible to the colds, flu, and other illnesses caused by these germs.

Bacteria and viruses find it easier to take hold in your body when your system is lacking important nutrients. Nutrients that bolster the immune system are vitamins A, C, and E, and essential fatty acids. The most important minerals include manganese, selenium, zinc, copper, iron, sulfur, magnesium, and germanium.

Consuming too many processed foods, sugar, and soda can weaken the body's immune system. Eating the wrong type of fats (hydrogenated oils, as found in deep-fried foods, margarine, and baked goods) can predispose your two-year-old to recurrent infections and inflammatory conditions. Sugar has also been shown to reduce the cell count of white blood cells, which fight and destroy germs that can cause disease.

The most nutrient-rich diet is supplied by organic whole foods, which include organically farmed meats and fish, fresh fruits and vegetables, nuts, seeds, beans, and whole grains. Essential fatty acids (the good fats) are also essential to normal immune and nervous system function. These are found in flaxseed oil, evening primrose oil, hemp seed oil, borage seed oil, and fish oil.

Sun Safety

Another important habit you must develop to protect your child's health now and into the future is the regular use of sunscreen (in conjunction with hats and other protective clothing). The best sunscreens for children are made with zinc oxide or titanium dioxide. These ingredients sit on top of the skin, forming a barrier against the sun's rays.

Sunblocks made with zinc oxide or titanium dioxide are known as *broad-spectrum* types, which means they protect against both UVA and UVB rays. The sun protection factor (SPF) should be at least fifteen, though it's not necessary to go any higher than thirty.

Broad-spectrum sunblocks offer the further advantage that they start protecting your child as soon as you put them on, unlike other types that need to be applied thirty minutes before you go outside (so the skin has time to absorb them).

 **Alert!**

Try to use sunscreen labeled PABA-free, because the amino acid PABA (para-aminobenzoic acid) can cause skin irritation. On the other hand, if this is the only sunscreen you have, go ahead and use it, since a negative reaction to PABA is less damaging to the skin than a sunburn.

No matter what kind of sunscreen you use, don't be stingy with it. Make sure that every body part is coated well, paying special attention to your child's ears, nose, back of the neck, feet, and shoulders. Do not put sunscreen near her eyes, because if it gets into her eyes, it will burn. Instead, have your two-year-old wear a hat and even sunglasses to protect the delicate eyelid and undereye area.

Some of the newer sunscreens appear brightly tinted when you first apply them and then fade to clear after a few minutes. This might reassure you that you've covered every inch of your child.

You need to reapply sunscreen every two hours, no matter what the label says about how long an application lasts. And always reapply sunscreen after your child has been in the water, even if the product is waterproof.

Insect Repellents

With their strong scents and scary-sounding ingredients, insect repellents are often worrisome for parents. Although products containing DEET work longer and are somewhat stronger than other repellents, these are not approved for very young children. In fact, the American Academy of Pediatrics recommends that even older children not use insect repellents containing more than 10 percent DEET. Keep in mind that if you are traveling to an area where insect-borne diseases such as malaria are prevalent, DEET-based repellents are the best protection and should be used as necessary.

Dressing your two-year-old in light-colored clothing that covers as much of her skin as possible also helps protect her from mosquitoes, flies, and other biting insects.

Repellents that contain citronella and other natural ingredients are generally a safe choice for children. These formulas work for only about two hours (or less) and then need to be reapplied.

Basic First Aid

Watching your two-year-old walking unsteadily as she investigates everything at eye level in her surroundings, you are undoubtedly aware that a knowledge of basic first aid is essential to ensure your child's health.

 Essential

> You should always keep a fully stocked first-aid kit in your home and be familiar with basic first-aid techniques, such as when to apply pressure to wounds and how to stop bleeding; what to do in case of poisoning; how to clean and dress a wound; and how to recognize a cut that needs stitches.

Most injuries that befall a two-year-old are of the everyday variety: scrapes, bumps, and bruises. With a knowledge of basic first aid, you can care for your child's common injuries yourself. If you do have a true emergency on your hands, you can administer first-aid techniques at once to reduce a chance of greater problems.

Bandages

If you head to the drugstore in search of children's Band-Aids, you'll find products galore decorated with lots of TV and movie characters. But you might also discover what parents have learned over the years: Those child-sized bandages don't cover most children's cuts and scrapes. Just because children's bodies are small doesn't mean their injuries are. If available, buy both adult and child-sized Band-Aids so you can mix and match. The fun decorations will make your child happy, but the proper-sized bandage will enable you to take proper care of her.

You also need gauze, surgical tape, and antiseptic cream to apply to your child's cuts and scrapes. You should have tweezers on hand for splinters, scissors to cut bandages or gauze, if necessary, and safety pins to wrap cloth around injuries.

Creams and Lotions

Besides antiseptic cream, you should have calamine lotion to stop itching, antibiotic cream to fight infection, and unscented moisturizer to put on your child's skin if it gets too dry. You should also have hydrocortisone cream on hand for itching and swelling.

Red-Flag Symptoms

Even when small children are running around seemingly healthy, they often have symptoms that require your attention—runny noses, coughs, low-grade fevers. A two-year-old won't blow or wipe his nose, he won't cover his mouth when he coughs, and most likely he won't tell you he wants to take it easy because he feels like he's coming down with an ailment. As an adult, you are able to recognize the initial symptoms of colds and other minor illnesses and as a result can treat these early on, often avoiding illness.

Similarly, in order to maintain your two-year-old's good health you need to know her body as intimately as your own, recognizing the first sign of illness through changes in her body or behavior. When you notice your child not being herself—whether this is reflected in her energy level, her sleeping pattern, eating habits, mood, or just by the way she looks (red eyes, dark circles under her eyes, pale skin, for example)—you can assume she's not feeling well.

Lethargy

When a toddler suddenly doesn't have the energy to get out of bed or he just wants to sit on the couch, there's a good chance he's sick. Lethargy can take the form not only of a need to sleep but of an inability to wake up and be alert. If your two-year-old is not moving about and seems to need you to hold him more than usual, he's likely not well and should see a doctor.

Holding the Ear

If your child tugs his ear or shakes his head a lot, he might have an ear infection. A two-year-old can't always tell you that his ear hurts, so he'll touch it rather than communicate in words. If he's crying a lot, he may also be in pain. Remember, an earache more often presents with a dull throbbing than with acute pain. Unlike a "boo-boo" that a two-year-old can recognize as an injury, earache pain may be difficult for your two-year-old to describe.

Breathing Problems

Breathing problems usually develop over time from a cold or exposure to an allergen. If your child develops a cough or congestion that evolves into difficulty breathing, meaning that he is taking shallow breaths, can't catch his breath, or is gasping for breath, you must take him to the doctor or an emergency room immediately. If your child's breathing becomes audible, that is another sign something is wrong. Not being able to catch his breath often scares a child, so try to keep him calm; anxiety or nervousness will make his breathing even more shallow. If you take deep breaths in front of him he may be able to imitate you, and that will help him calm down. Many breathing problems manifest as a cough that builds up over time. It is unusual for children to develop any of these breathing difficulties without some preceding symptoms like cough, fever, or runny nose. If your child has a cough that progresses to the point of him vomiting and having difficulty breathing, you should call your doctor immediately.

Always trust your own judgment in deciding whether to take your child to the doctor. It is always better to be concerned enough to seek help (even if nothing proves to be wrong) than to wait to seek treatment until your child is terribly ill.

Chapter 11

Common Illnesses and Symptoms

Your two-year-old is more predictable to you now than she used to be. You know, for example, the difference between her behavior when she's overtired and when she's unhappy. In addition to noticing your child's atypical behavior, you should be aware of common childhood illnesses and their symptoms so you can assess the situation if your two-year-old should exhibit signs of illness. Having a more informed understanding of your child's medical condition can be helpful in supplementing your doctor's knowledge and care.

Asthma

The rate of asthma in young children has increased significantly in recent years, affecting between 10 to 12 percent of all children. Children who suffer from asthma are almost always diagnosed before the age of five. Allergy-prone children are more likely to develop asthma, particularly if other members of their family suffer from asthma, eczema, or allergies. Children are also likely to develop asthma if they are exposed to smoking (before or after birth). Impoverished African-American male children in particular show a significant susceptibility to asthma.

Although it is unclear exactly why asthma rates are increasing, there are many ways parents can help their children with asthma feel better. It is especially important to follow your doctor's directions because lifestyle factors, including variables of diet, sleep, and exercise, can greatly affect your child's quality of life. Today, there are many medications available that control children's asthma better than in days past, leading to fewer attacks and consequently far less frequent emergency room visits.

Symptoms of Asthma

Parents can usually recognize the most obvious sign of asthma in their child: difficulty in breathing, wheezing, or having trouble taking a deep breath. But there are other, less well-known signs of asthma, including frequent coughing, especially at night or when laughing. If your child has trouble staying energetic when he plays or if he coughs during exercise and at night, you should bring him to the doctor. If you can see your two-year-old's chest and stomach moving deeply when he breathes, you should also talk to your doctor.

Helping Your Child Cope with Asthma

The severity of asthma symptoms in your child can be strongly affected by the choices you make. If you or others in your family smoke, you are exacerbating your child's symptoms. If you keep him confined to the house, he will probably feel worse. If you have pets, the dander may make his breathing more difficult.

 Fact

Most asthma symptoms can be kept under control so that your child can live a normal, healthy life. What matters most is a proactive, positive attitude combined with knowledge about how to live with asthma.

Because of the close relationship between asthma symptoms and lifestyle, doctors and families often work together to create an asthma action plan. This combines treatment with medications and the assistance of breathing apparatuses such as nebulizers and inhalers, which help provide oxygen to someone who isn't breathing properly.

Allergies

An allergy is an abnormally high sensitivity to certain substances such as pollens, foods, or micro-organisms. Common indications of allergy can include sneezing, itching, swelling, and skin rashes.

Fifteen to 20 percent of Americans have an allergy of one type or another (for example, food, animal, pollen), and most sufferers are diagnosed during childhood. Children whose family members have allergies are likely to have them, too, though the nature of the allergy in each case may be completely different. That is, if a mom is allergic to dogs, her child may be allergic to cats. In any case, if a parent has allergies, she needs to be aware that her child is also liable to have them. Of course, when a child has an allergy it is up to a parent to keep it under control.

 Alert!

> If your two-year-old has an allergy and is going on a play date, notify the adult in charge. If her allergies are extensive or require special care, make sure a list of her allergies accompanies her. That way her caregivers will know how best to handle an emergency or which foods she should avoid.

Hay fever, an allergy to pollen from hay and grasses that usually occurs in spring and summer, is the most common allergy. It consists of an irritation of the mucus membranes, which are located in the nose, mouth, eyes, and nasal cavity. Hay fever symptoms include itchy and watery red eyes, sneezing, and runny nose. Because your two-year-old suffering from hay fever can't yet blow her runny nose to clear her head, mucus drips down her throat, causing her to cough. Children, like adults, can also be allergic to dust, airborne particles, and pet dander from animals in their immediate environment.

To help your two-year-old be more comfortable during allergy season, try to minimize her exposure to allergens. This might mean keeping her inside with air conditioning on sunny days or keeping her away from the family pet (if you're able to still keep a pet).

There are many good allergy medications available for young children that won't make them drowsy or cause negative side effects. If you think your two-year-old has allergies, take her to the doctor for diagnosis. You may need to try a few medications, including varying the dosage, to find what is most effective for your child. Work with your doctor to come up with a treatment plan.

Rashes and Skin Allergies

There are a number of common rashes you might see on your two-year-old's skin. Most are not serious and are easily treated with over-the-counter cortisone and anti-itch cream. Even if the rash goes away quickly, however, it's important to determine its cause. Most likely it indicates an allergy of some kind whose recurrence you can prevent once you've identified the trigger.

Some rashes that usually show up as small red dots are caused by laundry products or other chemicals that might be on clothes. If you notice a rash on your child's back, chest, or arms, try changing detergents to one that is fragrance free. You might also switch soaps, shampoos, or other cleansers.

Fact

> Warts are caused by a common virus. They are usually white with a small brown dot in the middle. Although these are contagious, they aren't dangerous. Don't use an over-the-counter wart medicine on your child without consulting your doctor.

Your child's skin becomes dry and chapped when it's cold and dry out or if her baths are too hot. You'll know if your two-year-old has dry skin because the skin appears white and cracked. You can protect her skin in a few ways. First, make sure bath water is warm, not hot. When your child gets out of the bath, put lotion on her quickly, before the water evaporates off her skin.

Small children also commonly suffer from eczema, psoriasis, heat rash, and impetigo. If your child's skin erupts in blisters filled with pus, is exceedingly red and very itchy, or if the rash is causing bleeding, take her to the doctor. It's difficult for you as a parent to diagnose these skin problems on your own. A physician will be able to determine the cause of the problem and recommend the proper course of treatment.

Food Allergies

Food allergies, which are actually quite rare, often run in families. So if an adult in your family has an allergy to a food, you should be careful when you first give that food to your two-year-old. The most common foods that children are allergic to are milk, soy, egg, wheat, and nuts. If your child has a food allergy, the likelihood is that you learned about it when she was younger. Very few people are truly food-allergic for life. Most early food allergies actually go away as a child gets older. Some children have an intolerance for milk, which means they can't digest lactose. This also runs in families and is a lifelong condition, though it doesn't provoke an allergic reaction.

Anemia

Anemia occurs when a child doesn't have enough iron in his blood. People need iron in order to have energy and to feel good. Symptoms of iron deficiency include pale skin color, fatigue, irritability, brittle nails, unusual food cravings, and decreased appetite.

An iron-deficient diet is the most common cause of iron deficiency. Drinking too much cow's milk, such as more than a few glasses a day, is a classic cause of iron deficiency in young children, because cow's milk (which does not contain iron) inhibits absorption of iron from food. It is vital that your two-year-old eat a diet rich in iron. Iron-rich foods include spinach, beef, and broccoli. Pediatricians routinely test kids for anemia during well-child visits and check-ups.

Treatment of Anemia

If your two-year-old is anemic, most likely he will be prescribed oral iron supplements, which contain ferrous sulfate. Milk may interfere with absorption of iron and should not be taken at the same time as iron supplements. Vitamin C, essential in the production of hemoglobin, can increase iron absorption. Iron-rich foods include raisins, meats (liver is the highest source), fish, poultry, egg yolks, legumes (peas and beans), and whole-grain bread.

It is very important that your child not take too much iron in the form of vitamins—too much iron is as dangerous for him as too little.

The Need for Iron

Babies are born with about 500 mg of iron in their bodies. By the time they reach adulthood they need to have accumulated about 5000 mg. Your two-year-old needs to absorb an average of 1 mg per day of iron to keep up with the needs of his growing body. Since children only absorb about 10 percent of the iron they eat, most of them need to ingest 8–10 mg of iron per day.

Constipation and Diarrhea

A child tends to inherit the type of digestive system her parents have. There is no exact frequency with which a person should have bowel movements. Some people have them twice a day, others every two days. However, if your two-year-old has stomachaches or pains, has difficult bowel movements that include straining or pain, and passes hard balls of stool, or if she seems to be eating frequently but not having bowel movements with an appropriate frequency, then she is probably constipated. She may even indicate that she wants to have a bowel movement but is unable to produce one.

 **Alert!**

Never give your child a laxative without first checking with your doctor, because dosage is an important aspect of treating constipation; you don't want her digestive system to get out of sync. Most physicians use milder methods to facilitate children's bowel movements, such as glycerin suppositories or mineral oil.

Even though constipation is not a sign of illness, it makes your child uncomfortable, so you should try to correct it by giving her a varied diet and more water to drink. Make sure she eats a variety of foods, including fruits and vegetables. Portions that are the correct size for her body will help keep her digestive system regular.

Some good foods that help adjust a constipated digestive system include a few prunes, dried apricots or grapes, as well as oatmeal and green vegetables.

Diarrhea, the direct opposite of constipation (too many and very loose bowel movements), will not only upset your two-year-old, it can also hurt and cause her to become dehydrated and lethargic. Diarrhea may be caused by a virus, by contaminated food, or can sometimes be a side effect of medications. If diarrhea begins quickly but stops after the next meal your child eats and isn't accompanied by fever, you probably don't need to worry about it. But if it lasts for two days or your child seems weak and lethargic, take her to the doctor.

One common and effective way to treat diarrhea is with certain foods. Banana, white toast, and white rice have all been known to settle the stomach. You can also give your child an electrolyte drink for children (such as Pedialyte) to help replenish her fluids. However, stay away from ginger ale and other soda because the sugar in these may further upset her stomach.

Coughs and Colds

You know your two-year-old has a cold when he has a runny nose, sneezes a lot, seems to have trouble swallowing, and generally be congested. He'll probably cough a lot, too, because the mucus is running down his throat. More than 110 distinct viruses are known to cause the common cold.

If your child has a cold, it is important for him to drink more fluids than usual. You should also let him eat as much—or as little—as he likes. Medicine does not work on viruses, but one thing that does seem to help is soup. Although soup won't kill the virus, it will soothe your child's sore throat, clear his nasal passages, and combat dehydration. The hot soup produces steam that can help break up nasal congestion and keep his nasal passages moist.

If you are worried that your child may have influenza (the flu) rather than the common cold, consult the symptoms in the following table.

Cold symptoms

Mild fever, if any

Slight headache, if any

No aches and pains

Energy level relatively normal

Flu symptoms

High fever

Severe headache

Severe aches and pains

Extreme fatigue

When your two-year-old has the flu, he will typically be very tired and have a high fever (but not have cold symptoms). The flu can be dangerous, so if your child is lethargic and running a high fever, you should call your doctor to see if you should take him in. The flu is treated similarly to colds, and your child may need pain relievers to reduce his fever and ease his aches.

 Essential

One effective, old-fashioned remedy for congestion is a mentholated or eucalyptus-based chest rub, which clears the nasal and chest passages for easier breathing. A humidifier also comes in handy when your child is sick and having trouble breathing and sleeping.

Coughing is the body's way of removing foreign substances and mucus from the lungs and upper airway passages. Symptomatic coughs are often useful, and you should not try to eliminate them. If your two-year-old can't breathe or sleep because of a cough, however, you need to make him more comfortable by keeping him propped up in bed.

Drinking fluids may help thin secretions and soothe an irritated throat.

Dry, hacking coughs may respond to honey or lemon juice in hot water. Elevate your child's head with extra pillows at night to ease a dry cough. Your two-year-old is too young to suck on a cough drop, but you can offer him cough syrup to soothe his throat. No cough medicine has been proven to be totally effective for coughs, but if you find something that works for your child, use it.

Viruses

A number of childhood illnesses are due to infections, which are either bacterial or viral. It is hard to tell the difference between an illness caused by bacteria and one caused by viruses. Doctors often use a process of elimination to rule out a bacterial infection that can be treated with antibiotics. Most infections in humans are viruses—and antibiotics are useless against them.

Whereas bacterial infections can be threatening to our bodies and therefore require medical treatment, in general people recover easily from viruses. Some common infections that are all caused by different viruses include:

- chickenpox
- the common cold
- Coxsackie
- croup
- Fifth Disease

- the flu
- measles
- mononucleosis
- mumps
- stomach flu or gastroenteritis

There are also fungal infections, such as ringworm and candida diaper rash. Parasitic infections include head lice, scabies, and pinworms.

Many times it is difficult to distinguish between a viral infection and a bacterial infection, which is why your doctor needs to examine your child if he is sick, possibly running some tests in order to diagnose your child's symptoms properly.

Diagnosis

As you can see from the list of potential illnesses—and from knowing that most children go through their lives without contracting the majority of these—it is impractical and somewhat unnecessary to explain each one. Instead, you just need to know that in general, a fever of 101°F or lower is likely to be viral rather than bacterial. Even a high fever of 102°F or above is probably viral as well, but it brings an increased risk of a bacterial infection. If your two-year-old has a fever in combination with other visible signs of illness, such as a rash, then you should call your doctor. Many infections have specific symptoms, such as a rash around the nose (impetigo) or a very congested chest (pneumonia). Explaining the specific symptoms to your doctor will help you both treat your child properly.

Croup

Croup—a hacking, barking cough—is very common in young children. In all likelihood, you have already spent a few nights in a steamy bathroom or out in the cold air with your coughing two-year-old, helping him breathe easier.

Pediatricians treat croup in different ways. Some prescribe a steroid, prednisone, to reduce the swelling in the throat so that your child recovers faster. Antibiotics do not work for croup. Others will have you tough it out with your child for a few days. Croup usually is bad for one night, gets worse the next, then starts to get better, and is gone within a few days after that.

 Question

> **How can I ease my two-year-old's croup symptoms at night?**
> Take him outside to breathe drier, cooler air, or if it's cold out crack a window and prop him up with warm clothes and blankets near the window. You can also try using a humidifier to see whether the steam helps.

As upsetting as it can be to hear your two-year-old cough like a seal, he is often able to ignore his symptoms and get through the day just fine. your child may get upset if he is unable to sleep at night. In that case, you may need to give him some acetaminophen, which might help him relax and ease his fever a bit. Even with scary episodes of croup in which your child is gasping for air and making honking noises, he will often recover after breathing cool air. Despite the best efforts of parents, some children do get into severe respiratory difficulty and need to be taken to the emergency room. Although a child is often better by the time he arrives, the emergency room doctor may see fit to treat him with a steroid injection to ward off further episodes.

Conjunctivitis

There are three types of conjunctivitis, also known as pinkeye: viral, allergic, and bacterial. With the exception of allergic conjunctivitis, this condition is typically contagious. The viral type often occurs with an upper respiratory tract infection, a cold, or a sore throat. The allergic type occurs seasonally. Allergic conjunctivitis may also be caused by intolerance to substances such as cosmetics, perfumes, or drugs. Infection usually begins with one eye, but may spread easily to the other eye.

The signs of each type of conjunctivitis are the same: red eyes and watery discharge, itching, and swollen eyelids. A stringy discharge that may cause the eyelids to stick together, especially after sleeping, is another telltale sign of conjunctivitis.

Conjunctivitis in your two-year-old requires a doctor's care because, depending on what type it is, eye drops must be prescribed. Bacterial conjunctivitis is usually treated with antibiotic eye drops or ointments that cover a broad range of bacteria. Cool compresses often relieve the discomfort of pinkeye until you can get to the doctor. If your child has pinkeye, she should not be allowed to swim in a pool because some bacteria can be spread through the water.

Vomiting

Another common symptom of illness in two-year-olds is vomiting. Vomiting is usually the first symptom of a stomach virus that the body must expel. It is often followed by diarrhea, which (especially in combination with vomiting) can put your child at risk for dehydration.

Vomiting is most often caused by viruses, but it can also be caused by bacteria and parasites. Occasionally vomiting can be caused by serious intestinal problems (that is, appendicitis or abdominal obstructions) requiring surgery, but these are rare in two-year-olds. In such cases the vomiting is usually severe and unrelenting.

Cases of vomiting that follow a meal may be caused by esophageal reflux, but this is also unusual in two-year-olds. In addition to the danger of dehydration, vomiting can be very scary and exhausting for a child, and it can hurt. If your child has been vomiting, watch him to see if he is dehydrated. Your child is dehydrated if he looks pale, isn't urinating, has a dry mouth, cracked lips, and is very thirsty. His eyes may also look sunken.

Fluids to Supply

If your two-year-old has long bouts of vomiting or diarrhea, he needs to drink fluids to replace those lost from vomiting. If you suspect dehydration, you should talk to your doctor. In the meantime, encourage your child to drink an oral rehydration solution (ORS), such as Pedialyte, which contains the right mix of salt, sugar, potassium, and other elements to help replace lost body fluids. If your child won't drink Pedialyte (it is very salty), try to flavor it with Gatorade or another electrolyte sports drink. Encourage him to drink water, watered-down juice (too much sugar might upset his stomach), and chicken broth.

Foods That Help

If your two-year-old is vomiting, try giving him small amounts of ORS, such as one teaspoonful every five minutes. When he is able to keep the drink down, slowly increase the amount you give. If he keeps vomiting, wait thirty to sixty minutes after the last time he vomited, and then give him a few sips of ORS. Small amounts every few minutes may stay down better than a large amount all at once. When he stops vomiting, you can increase how much ORS you give each time and lengthen the time between drinks to three to four hours. Keep giving ORS until your child stops vomiting.

Once he's ready to eat again, try giving your child dry toast, small amounts of pasta without sauce, a hard-boiled egg, rice, or a banana. It will take a few days for his appetite to return to normal. Don't force him to eat, but make sure he has plenty to drink. Remember, it is often difficult to judge dehydration. When in doubt, contact your pediatrician.

Ear Infections

Acute otitis media is an infection of the middle ear and is one of the most common illnesses of childhood. There are two different types of otitis media—viral and bacterial—that can occur in one or both ears at the same time. Ten to 20 percent of children will have otitis media three or more times, with fluid staying in their ears an average of one month each time.

When your two-year-old has a cold, the eustachian tube between the ear and the throat can become blocked, causing fluid to build up in the middle ear. The virus can become trapped in this fluid and multiply, causing infection. You can tell your child has an ear infection when she pulls on her ear, has drainage from the ear, has a fever (with acute otitis media), or has trouble sleeping. Talk to your pediatrician if these symptoms occur.

 Fact

All children have an amazing amount of ear wax. Children probably produce the same amount of ear wax as adults, but then they also have tinier ears. Don't worry too much about ear wax. Clean only what you can see. If there is a problem with the wax, your doctor will help with removal in the office or can recommend wax softeners for use at home.

Your child may have all, some, or none of these symptoms and still have otitis media. Ear infections can be treated by antibiotics prescribed by your doctor. The fever and pain should decrease within two days, but you must continue administering the prescribed medication until all of it is gone.

Hearing Problems

If your child has fluid in her middle ear, the fluid reduces sound traveling through the part of the ear such that sound may be muffled or not heard. Children with middle-ear fluid will generally have a mild or moderate temporary hearing loss. (It feels like you've plugged your ears with your fingers.)

Most problems with otitis media arise during a child's first three years, which coincide with the period when she is learning to speak and to understand words. It may be harder to hear and understand speech if sound is muffled by fluid in the middle ear. Special attention needs to be paid to language development if your child has fluid, because if your child has difficulty hearing as a result of fluid, you may realize it when she misses developmental milestones.

At two, your child should be able to do the following:

- Understand differences in meaning (*go* versus *stop*, *big* versus *little*)
- Follow a two-step sequence (such as, "Get the book and put it on the table.")
- Use two- to three-word phrases to talk about and ask for things
- Ask for or direct attention to objects by naming them

Tubes and Surgery Options

If your two-year-old has a lot of ear infections or fluid is present in both ears for four to six months, your doctor may recommend that she have surgery to place a tube in her ear.

This tube allows air to enter the middle-ear space. The procedure, performed by an ear, nose, and throat doctor, helps the lining of the middle ear return to normal and prevents new infections. The tube generally stays in place for six to twelve months and then falls out by itself. Talk with your child's doctor if you think there is a need for these treatments.

Fever

As in an adult, a child's normal body temperature is 98.6°F. If your two-year-old's temperature goes above 100.4°F, then he is considered to have a fever. Keep in mind that forehead and ear temperatures are not very accurate. Mouth, underarm, and rectal temperatures, though varying somewhat from each other, are the most accurate ways of determining your child's temperature and state of wellness.

Fevers do not always have to be treated. If your child's fever is under 101°F and he seems fine—alert, happy, and his typical self—then you can let it run its course. If it lasts more than a day, though, call your pediatrician and describe the symptoms accompanying the fever. Your child may benefit from a fever reducer, such as acetaminophen, ibuprofen, or a combination of the two to keep him comfortable. (Some pediatricians recommend alternating age- and weight-appropriate dosages of each.) Take his temperature every couple of hours when he's sick; let your doctor know if it goes higher than 103°F, if he is shaking or shivering as well as feverish, or if he seems delusional.

Most fevers are short-lived and do not get very high. Even if they do get high at night, they are often lower during the day and run their course within a day. Fevers break suddenly and then temperature returns to normal.

Pain Relief

A child's bones, muscles, and even skin grow so quickly that the growth sometimes seems to happen overnight. These rapid changes can be painful, which your child may feel especially at night in her legs. If your two-year-old complains that her legs hurt, try giving her a pain reliever to help her sleep and see how she feels in the morning. If her walking or posture then seems affected, call your pediatrician. But if she seems to feel better, then assume she is experiencing growing pains. This doesn't usually last more than two nights in a row.

When your child has a fever, is achy, has growing pains, or has a sore throat, she may benefit from a pain reliever. Information about the three main types of pain reliever follows.

- **Acetaminophen** – Tylenol and similar medications are effective for reducing pain and can make your child more comfortable if she has a fever
- **Ibuprofen** – Advil, Motrin, and other medications with ibuprofen reduce pain and discomfort from fever. Ibuprofen is also an anti-inflammatory and might help the discomfort associated with growing pains
- **Aspirin** – Young children should never take aspirin or aspirin derivatives such as Excedrin.

Aspirin and aspirin derivatives can be harmful to a small child and can lead to Reyes syndrome, a severe neurological complication of chicken pox and the flu. This syndrome occurs when those illnesses are treated with aspirin. Because doctors often don't know what illness a child is coming down with, it is best to avoid giving aspirin for any of your child's illnesses.

Acetaminophen and ibuprofen for children are the same medications as those for adults but in lower doses. They are usually in liquid, gel, or soluble form since two-year-olds cannot swallow pills (and shouldn't be expected to). You can buy generic brands of these medications and be assured they are safe and effective. Never give your child adult versions of medications, because children can easily overdose or get sick from too much medication. Sometimes these medications will have a slight tranquilizing effect on your child. It is very important that you use pain relievers only when your child is uncomfortable and sick, not to help her sleep or relax. Pain medications can be overused and dangerous if directions are not followed.

Chapter 12

A Safe Environment

The first rule of safety in taking care of your two-year-old is: Don't take your eyes off her! Two-year-olds will run around stores, playgrounds, and the backyard faster than seems possible. Just because your child is more physically independent now that she's two doesn't mean she is more aware of her surroundings. You have to keep her safe without making her overly cautious or frightened of what can happen to her. This requires a delicate balance on your part, but you'll be rewarded with a secure child who is familiar with the practice of limit-setting and safe behavior.

Car Seats

A two-year-old needs to sit in a car seat any time she is going for a ride. Your child probably still fits in the car seat she has used ever since outgrowing her infant seat as a three-month-old. No particular style is the best overall or the safest, nor is price necessarily indicative of safety. What matters is that your car seat fits your child and is installed properly.

All car safety seats sold in the United States must meet very strict safety standards set by the federal government. When you shop for a car seat, put your child in it and adjust the harnesses and buckles. Then make sure the seat fits properly and securely in your car. At two, your child should be in a forward-facing seat, which is available in the form of convertible seats, built-in seats, and combination forward-facing/booster seats. Whatever type of seat you buy, you need to use it every time your child is in the car, making sure she is held in very securely, with all of the straps fastened and the locks closed.

 Alert!

Always have your two-year-old ride with the car seat in the back seat, and always wear your own seat belt. Never leave your child alone in the car, even if you're just running into the store "for a second." Your child is not safe left alone at this age, and your car might easily be hit by another car or stolen.

There are two things to remember when securing your child in a car seat:

1. Your child must be buckled snugly into the seat.
2. The car seat must be buckled tightly in place in the back seat.
3. The car seat should also rest tightly *against* the back seat so that it can't wiggle or move if it is jostled.

Your car may need a harness, locking clips, or straps to keep the car seat from moving on impact. Locking clips are not needed in most newer vehicles, but some seat belts (especially those found in older cars) need a special heavy-duty locking clip that is available only from the car manufacturer.

Also, the straps should be firm against your two-year-old's body. No blankets or heavy coats should come between your toddler and the straps, since this might create an illusion of security (because your child could get loose in event of an accident).

Each car safety seat is different. Read the instructions that come with your seat and keep them handy in the glove compartment. Follow the manufacturer's instructions at all times. If you need help installing your car seat, go to *www.seatcheck.org* to get the name of a local car safety expert.

Home Safety

A two-year-old is not too young to start learning about safety. Your lessons should be delivered calmly and without focusing on the danger itself. Don't emphasize to your child how she might get hurt, but instead teach her how to stay safe. Say, for example, "You need to sit down in the tub, because it's slippery" rather than, "You're going to fall! Stop standing up!" You thus provide your child with a positive set of instructions as well as an explanation of why you're giving her these specific directions.

 Essential

> Be sure to keep electrical outlets covered, because toddlers will try to put their fingers (or objects) into them. Be sure wires and cords are secured so your two-year-old can't pull down a lamp, stereo, TV, or piece of electronic equipment.

If you want to reinforce a safety lesson, ask your child to teach you what you've just been teaching her. Give her a favorite doll or stuffed animal, asking her to pretend the doll is taking a bath. "How can you take care of your doll in the bath?" You can use this approach with all safety lessons.

Sharp Corners

When an unsteady toddler runs through the house without paying attention to her surroundings, she can easily fall and hit her head (or arm or leg) on the corner of a table, radiator, staircase, fireplace, or piece of furniture. If you have very sharp edges in your house, be sure to cover them with corner protectors (foam pads that stick to your furniture).

Toddlers often hit their heads on low tables, door knobs, the edges of chairs, and fireplaces. Remember, their heads are lower to the ground than yours, so though you might bump your knee on a chair, they will bump their nose or forehead. Two-year-olds have hard heads so bumps and falls from their height are usually harmless. Falls from higher heights are more dangerous, of course. As your child moves about the house, watch her in order to notice which objects are at her eye level so you can protect her from them.

If your child often plays in one or two particular rooms, minimize the amount of furniture she could run into. Make sure she has enough space to play the way she likes without hurting herself. You can start to teach her about areas of your home that are not safe for her to play in, such as the kitchen (near the appliances), or near the fireplace. Teach her also to stay away from burning candles. Never leave your two-year-old alone in a room with a burning candle.

Stairs

Even when they are confident—and with good reason—about their walking skills, toddlers can easily slip or trip on steps. Staircase safety is very important because a child could fall down an entire flight of stairs if she overlooks a step near the top.

Safety gates can be secured across the top of a staircase prevent such accidents. Also consider getting staircase treads if you have hard wooden steps (which can be extra slippery). Your steps should have a railing that is easy for your child to hold onto as she walks up and down the stairs.

Cabinet Locks

A two-year-old is nothing if not independent and curious, so if she sees a closed cabinet or door, she's going to try to open it and explore what's inside. Cabinets often hold dangerous items, including medicine, utensils, and cleaning products. To prevent your two-year-old from exploring the potentially dangerous contents of your household cabinets, it is essential that you purchase and install cabinet locks. You can buy cabinet locks in most hardware stores or through childproofing Web sites like *www.totsafe.com* and *www.safe beginnings.com*.

It is crucial to have a lock system in place if you have a gun in the house. If you do keep a gun at home, keep it out of sight and out of reach of your child. All guns should be kept locked and unloaded, with their ammunition stored separately.

 Alert!

Guns are kept in nearly half of all households in the United States. Even if you don't own one, you can't always know whether the home your child visits has one. So it's vital to instruct your two-year-old about how dangerous guns are—and what to do if she comes across one.

No matter what your position on having guns, all children should learn the following rules from the National Rifle Association (NRA) about what to do if they come in contact with a gun:

- Stop
- Don't touch
- Leave the area
- Tell an adult

It's particularly important that your child know to leave any room that has a gun, especially if she is with another child who could accidentally pull a trigger. A three-year-old has enough strength to pull the trigger of a gun. Your child needs to know that she must always tell an adult if she or a friend has a found a gun.

Bathrooms

Although most burns occur in the kitchen, children can also be burned if the water from a sink or bathtub faucet is too hot. Your home should have the water heater temperature set at no more than 75°F. Consider putting faucet covers on the bathtub and sinks (especially those your two-year-old uses frequently) so that she can't turn the faucets on by herself.

Water and Pool Safety

Many parents believe their two-year-old can swim when, in reality, their child isn't actually swimming. Just because a small child may be able to move in the water doesn't mean he is consciously keeping himself afloat. Moving in the water is an instinct for some babies, but paddling is not the same as swimming—and does not guarantee that a child's head will stay above water.

A child can drown in a moment even in very shallow water because he can't always pick up his head if he should fall. Or he could panic and not remember to pick up his head. An adult—not an older child—needs to be in the water accompanying a two-year-old at all times. This rule applies not only to pools, but to any body of shallow water, whether the ocean's edge, a lake, a toddler pool, or a bathtub.

Pools should be covered and fenced off, and motion detectors and sensors, in case small children go in or fall in when no one is looking. These sensors are available at hardware stores, pool-supply stores, and Web sites that sell child-safety equipment, such as *www.childsafetystore.com*.

Many two-year-olds enjoy playing in kiddie pools, which are small plastic pools you can buy at most pool and toy stores and that you fill with a garden hose. Do not leave your child unattended near a kiddie pool. Have him wear water wings in the pool if he wants to try to swim or float. Always empty the pools when you're not using them. That way your child can't happen to wander over to it and fall in while you are distracted, and you won't be leaving the pool to fill with dirty water. (Chlorine for killing germs is not used in kiddie-pool water.)

Stranger Danger

Keeping your child safe from strangers is another area that demands you walk a fine line. On the one hand, you don't want your child to be afraid of people. You want him to be friendly, courteous, and naturally trusting. On the other hand, two-year-olds do not understand what a stranger is and are inclined to do whatever any adult tells them to (which is a scary prospect to any parent).

An essential habit you need to instill in your two-year-old is that he shouldn't be afraid to yell and scream if someone hurts him, no matter who it is. Teaching your child to use a loud voice as a defensive measure gives him the ability to fight back should he ever feel threatened.

 Fact

It is not only strangers who can hurt your child. Family members are statistically the ones most likely to hurt a young child. If you sense that someone is hurting your two-year-old, listen to your instincts and keep him away from that person, or else alert authorities. Convey to your child that you are on his side no matter what.

You can further protect your two-year-old by teaching him his name and your name. Emphasize that he should never go anywhere without you first giving him permission. Tell him that even if someone else says it's okay, that isn't enough; the okay needs to come from you. Inform your child of each day's schedule so he knows what situations to expect. That will help him recognize when something has gone awry (such as getting lost or being approached by a threatening person).

Understand the Statistics

Unfortunately parents hear a lot of scary stories about children being abducted, even right from their own bedrooms, by strangers. This scenario is incredibly rare. The stories you hear may be frightening, but they are really uncommon. As a matter of fact, children are most often hurt by their parents. So—as upsetting as this may be to hear—if you or someone you care about is in danger of hurting your child, get help for everyone involved. Most adults who hurt their children don't intend to commit a crime; they simply need support and training to learn how to parent better.

Be Realistic

If you are in a mall, a store, or even in your house and you can't find your two-year-old, don't get hysterical, but do take action immediately. Notify someone nearby, such as a store clerk or a companion, then yell for your child. Sometimes a child will hide in a store as a game, so yell out, "I found you! Come out!" Take care not to sound angry (since that will frighten your child). What is important is that you find him. Do not worry about overreacting, because if there is a problem you need to be able to spring into action. Still, you want to think clearly and be able to help those who come to your assistance.

Walking and Biking Safety

Children are at a higher risk than adults for pedestrian injuries because drivers can't see them as easily (especially a child standing between parked cars on the side of the road). Two-year-olds cannot judge whether it's safe to cross a street. Instead of waiting, they can run into the street without thinking.

Parents often overestimate their child's ability to cross the street. Don't cross the street and then yell for your two-year-old to join you. You should always be holding her hand. This is especially important in parking lots, where a person backing a car up can injure or hit a child who has been left unattended.

 Essential

When out walking with your two-year-old, demonstrate safe street-crossing by verbalizing what you are looking out for. At the street corner, stop and say, "Okay, we're going to be crossing the street. But first we have to stop, look both ways, and listen for cars." (The slogan *Stop, Look, and Listen!* is a helpful one for children to memorize.)

Stroller Safety

Strollers with children in them can topple over due to shopping bags weighing down the handles. Also, your child can slide out from the reclining back of a stroller without you noticing. Strollers seem safe because a child is (supposed to be) strapped in, but as with car seats, if they aren't used properly, they can become dangerous.

Always use the stroller's parking brake when putting your child in or taking him out. Once he's in the stroller, make sure he's strapped in with the seat belt or harness—even if you have to wake him up to strap him in.

Don't hang heavy purses, bags, or coats from the handles of a stroller; tuck them into the basket under the seat instead.

Also be sure never to leave your child alone in a stroller. If part of the stroller rips or breaks, get a new stroller.

At a minimum your child's stroller should have a strap that goes around your child's waist and another that goes between his legs. Even better is a five-point harness, which includes straps for the shoulder. Make sure the lap belt or harness is solidly attached to the frame of the stroller. If your child has a growth spurt, make sure you change the strap lengths so he stays secure.

To be safe, a stroller should have a wide base, so look for this feature even when buying an umbrella stroller. Even though the canopy of your stroller can protect your child from wind, rain, and sun, be aware that heat can build up inside a covered stroller. Keep an eye on your child's face to make sure he's not getting too warm sitting in a stroller.

Maintaining Safety Near the Street

When going out for a walk with your two-year-old, walk on the outside, and have your child walk on the inside. If there is no sidewalk, keep your two-year-old in a stroller. Always keep hold of your child's hand, because she could easily dart into the street or run into a yard with a dog, especially if she's a fearless toddler. Do not assume that because someone (the driver of a car, for example) can see you that they can see your child—they probably can't.

Bike Seat Precautions

You can take your child on bike rides using a bike seat or a trailer. Trailers are very stable, but cars will not always see them, so you should never take them in traffic. Trailers are also notoriously bumpy, so your two-year-old might have an unpleasant ride. Keep this in mind, especially if you approach a pothole—as your child will feel it much more than you.

If you take your two-year-old for bike rides—whether she's in a childseat or in a trailer behind you—she must wear a bicycle helmet. Not all children enjoy bicycles. If your child doesn't, don't force her to ride with you; you want her to have a positive association with bikes as she gets older.

Ensuring your two-year-old's health and safety is the most basic of your responsibilities. But the happiness you'll derive from all the rest that comes with being a parent—playing games, taking walks, reading stories, learning about all plants and animals—will more than compensate for whatever difficulties you face. This year requires a lot of care and oversight on your part, for your two-year-old will move faster than ever and be curious about everything. So make sure this year is a safe and fun time for you both!

Appendix A

Fun and Games
for Two-Year-Olds

When it comes to entertaining your two-year-old, creativity and knowledge will help you out immensely. You can encourage your two-year-old's imagination and help her learn by playing games and reading to her—rather than buying expensive toys. The following activities can help you entertain and play with your child, no matter what her interests are.

Animal Activities

Every child loves cute and soft animals: baby ducks, bunnies, and kittens. And some two-year-olds love all animals, even those that others find scary. There are lots of ways to play animal games, fortunately without spending money!

Activity 1: What Am I?

Make an animal noise and have your child guess what kind of animal you are. You can also get down on the floor and act like that animal. You and your child can take turns. Some animals that appeal to two-year-olds are:

- ducks
- sheep
- pigs
- monkeys
- dogs
- cats
- lions
- tigers
- bears
- frogs

Your child can also play an animal. Make sure you guess wrong sometimes. When your child barks, guess that she's a kitten. When she croaks like a frog, pretend you think she's a dog. This will make her think the game is fun for you, too, and she'll enjoy correcting your mistakes.

Activity 2: Animal Crowns

Two-year-olds don't always like to wear masks on their faces (although you can certainly try making some). As an alternative, you can make crowns with animal faces on the front, so your child can pretend to be an animal without covering his face.

1. To make the crown, cut strips of construction paper and tape them together so that they fit around your child's head.
2. Draw an animal face on another piece of construction paper. (This doesn't have to be perfect.) Another option is to cut pictures of animal faces out of magazines and glue them onto the crowns.
3. Tape or glue the animal face onto the strip that makes up the crown.

Activity 3: Animal Album

Get some old issues of science and nature magazines and make an animal scrapbook using the pictures. Your child will be able to look through the book whenever she wants. You can write the name of the animal and the noise it makes next to each picture.

Arts and Crafts

Two-year-olds don't have solid fine-muscle control, so their art projects have to be large and must not require a lot of careful work. Drawing isn't really something they can do yet. Your best bets are gluing (glue sticks are not as messy as white glue) and painting. When gluing, give your children large objects, such as feathers, pieces of felt, or paper, to attach to their work. Two-year-olds can also paint. The paintbrushes should also be large, or children can use their fingers. Keep in mind that your child will make a mess, so you may want to take these activities outside.

Activity 1: Homemade Clay

Mix together:

1 cup flour

1 cup boiling water

2 tbsp. cream of tartar

½ cup salt

1 tbsp. oil

Divide the clay into balls and add a drop or two of food coloring to each ball to make different colors.

Activity 2: Feathered Animal

You'll need feathers (which you can buy in drugstores and craft stores), glue or glue sticks, and construction paper to make this craft. Draw a bird or duck on the construction paper. You can leave the drawing as is, or you can have your two-year-old paint or color in the animal. Next, have her drip glue onto the drawing. Then let her stick the feathers on the glue so that the finished product resembles a feathered animal.

You can make this type of picture project with two-year-olds as long as you do the actual drawing, since they cannot make any kind of representational art. They are really just playing with the materials.

Activity 3: Making a Mural

Put up a laundry line outside, then drape a sheet over the line, and secure it with clothespins. The sheet should be low enough that your child can reach most of it himself. If you want, put a bathing suit on him and have a wading pool nearby. Fill cups with different colors of paints and include a large paintbrush for each. Let your child paint the sheet. She may want you to hang it up in the house once it's dry, but you might also use it as a tent. If you use fabric paint, then you'll be able to wash the sheet and use it as a tablecloth for future craft projects or a birthday party.

Cooking with Your Two-Year-Old

Most two-year-olds don't want to cook, but they do want to play with food. And yours will be very proud of any final creation when he helps you in the kitchen. For all of these activities start by washing your child's hands (and yours) and putting a drop cloth down on the floor to make cleanup easier.

Activity 1: Making Pizza

You can buy pizza dough and have your child help you roll it out. After you spread tomato sauce on top, put out bowls of toppings for your child to decorate the pizza with. Try cheese, cooked hamburger, tomato slices, olives, and mushrooms.

Activity 2: Making Fruit Salad

You can have your two-year-old help you make fruit salad by giving him tasks that he can do with his hands. Give him peeled bananas, which he can break into pieces, and peeled oranges, which he can break into segments. Have your child sprinkle in raisins and peeled, sliced apples. You can also try using cubes or slices of peaches, mango, papaya, kiwi, and other fruits. Your child can mix up the ingredients and put them in bowls for each member of the family.

Activity 3: Making Fruit Triangles

Buy puff pastry or refrigerated triangular rolls and divide the dough for your child into triangles. Have him spread teaspoons of jam on each triangle and top with another triangle. Make sure you pinch or stick the edges together (your child will try, but you need to make sure they are closed). Then bake for a delicious dessert!

Costumes

Two-year-olds enjoy dressing up, and the costumes they have fun wearing don't have to be complicated or expensive. Your child will enjoy just going through your drawers and closets for his supply of costumes—since that's the best way for him to pretend to be a grown-up. Don't be surprised if your daughter puts on a man's vest or if your son tries to wear high heels. Their preferences have nothing to do with gender and everything to do with imitating their parents.

Activity 1: Hats and Scarves

One of the easiest ways to let your child play with clothes is to give her hats (especially cowboy hats, fedoras, and big hats, which are lots of fun for two-year-olds). Pair the hat with some scarves, and she'll feel like a new person—someone grown-up and exciting! She'll especially like to dance and wave the scarves around, so make sure there is music playing.

Activity 2: Superhero Costume

A Spiderman, Buzz Lightyear, or Batman costume can cost $30, and your child may grow out of it before feel you got your money's worth. Your two-year-old can exercise his imagination by creating his own superhero costume. Supply him with tights or leggings, an interesting bathing suit, or pair of shorts, a mask (make one out of construction paper and string or a ribbon), and a cape (use a blanket or piece of old sheet)—and presto! You have your own original superhero.

Activity 3: Dressing Like Mom and Dad

If you have some old clothes, hand them over to your two-year-old and let her pretend to be you. She will especially love trying to walk in your shoes, wearing your sunglasses, and putting on your jackets, dresses, and pants.

Dancing and Music

Though dancing is one of those activities that often comes naturally to people, your two-year-old will feel more comfortable if you get up with him and dance. Because small children have a low center of gravity (which helps them balance), when they move or dance to music it often looks as if they don't have a natural sense of rhythm. But actually, most children love being sung to, love to sing, and love to play instruments.

For years, children's music was limited to songs that weren't very appealing to adults. These days, fortunately, lots of talented musicians are writing songs for young children. There are even online and broadcast radio shows specifically programmed for children, including "The Playground" on Emerson College Radio (*www.wers.org*) and "Kid's Corner" on University of Pennsylvania Radio (*www.wxpn.org*). You can also purchase or download music specifically for your two-year-old, including songs from PBS's *Sesame Street* and by performers who entertain children specifically, such as Laurie Berkner, Dan Zanes, and *The Wiggles*.

Activity 1: Follow the Leader

You can do this with or without music, and it's a great game for outside. (You can also do it inside when it's raining and your child can't run outdoors.) You start out as the leader, so your child learns how the game goes. Tell him to follow you. You can start out marching, then you can walk in different ways: backwards, sideways, waving your hands, or clapping. Two-year-olds can't always hop or skip, but you can certainly do it yourself and applaud your child's efforts if he tries to follow you. Don't forget to let him try being the leader.

Activity 2: Exploring Instruments

If you have any instruments in your house that aren't especially valuable to you, such as guitars and pianos, encourage your child to play them, gently. Many children appreciate being allowed to touch something they know belongs to their parents, and it's better to teach them how to treat an instrument than simply to forbid them from touching it. You can also purchase easy-to-play instruments, such as drums, bells, cymbals, a xylophone, a kazoo, or a triangle.

Activity 3: Singing Songs

"Twinkle Twinkle Little Star," "She'll Be Coming 'Round the Mountain," and "Row, Row, Row Your Boat" are all favorites of small children. Two-year-olds will often want to sing the same songs again and again, which is a challenge for you to bear since the songs themselves are already full of repetitive words. There are wonderful CDs with a variety of songs for children to help you provide your child with some variety, such as:

- *Doc Watson's Songs for Little Pickers*
- *The Bottle Let Me Down*
- *Classic Disney CDs*

Keep in mind, though, that you do not need to purchase any music at all. Singing your favorite songs to your child will make her just as happy.

Nature

It may seem silly, but some two-year-olds think a walk around the block is as exciting as a trek through the jungle. Being outside is not only interesting for a child, it is good for her. It gets her off the couch and out in the fresh air, gives her time to learn about the world, and is also beneficial for her mood and health.

Activity 1: Bug Collecting

Lots of stores sell bug collectors, which typically are wooden boxes with wire (so the bug can breathe and your child can see it). Though this is something you can easily make with your child, you could simply go on a bug hunt with a magnifying glass and a net. Your child can look at the bug, but you don't actually have to bring it home. Explain that the bug needs to be left alone in order to live, but like scientists, the two of you can examine the bug closely.

Activity 2: Leaf Collecting

Taking along a basket or grocery bag, go for a walk through the woods with your toddler. Have her pick up anything she wants (rocks, leaves, sticks). Promise that you will keep everything for a day or two so that she can look at what she collected when she's home. Leaf rubbings (made by placing a leaf under a piece of thin paper and rubbing over the paper with a crayon) are a little difficult for a two-year-old to do alone, but you can have her glue some of the smaller findings to construction paper.

Activity 3: Gardening

Getting your two-year-old a children's gardening set is a good investment—she will be able to rake, shovel, and dig near you in the garden without getting hurt (since such tools will be child-sized and made of plastic). If you don't encourage your child to dig along with you, she's unlikely to let you garden in peace. Give her some seeds (sunflower seeds are good) to put in the holes you dig together so that later she can watch them grow.

Princesses

Two-year-old girls often want to be princesses after watching movies and hearing fairy tales about kingdoms, adventures, and royal families, and some two-year-old boys will be interested in princesses as well. These activities for princess-loving children focus on exploring through imagination, which is constructive because otherwise princess lovers may watch too many videos if they don't find a way to engage that interest.

Activity 1: Build a Castle

Get a large box, such as the kind a refrigerator or another appliance comes in. Cut the top of the box into the shape of a castle tower by cutting small squares out of the top to create a crenelation. You can also cut a door on one side. This can be your princess' castle. You can also tape a bunch of open boxes together to make a larger castle.

Activity 2: Create a Princess Costume

If you have an old, flowing skirt, let your two-year-old wear that, or simply tuck some scarves into her tights or pants so that she has a flouncy skirt. Then make a crown out of construction paper. Covering a paper-towel roll in tin foil makes a scepter. Let your child wear a pair of your shoes.

Activity 3: Create a Princess Story

You can easily make up princess stories that are sure to entertain your two-year old. The basic princess story can be adapted to all kinds of situations and can incorporate any number of challenges to keep your child interested. You can model your story on this order of events: A girl is born a princess, something difficult happens (typically her mother dies and she inherits an evil stepmother, but you can think of something less Freudian, such as being afraid to swim across the moat or losing her crown), the princess tries to overcome the difficulty but fails, something difficult happens again, the princess tries to overcome the difficulty, and almost overcomes it, the princess has to try harder, and finally she succeeds. The success does not have to involve being rescued by a prince. For a great story about a princess who recognizes her true value—and the worthlessness of a superficial prince—read *The Paper Bag Princess* by Robert Munsch.

Sports

If you (or another adult in your household) regularly watch or play sports, your child will likely enjoy these activities as well. Of course, even if you don't enjoy sports, your child may like them anyway as she gets older. At the age of two, though, no matter what her exposure to actual sports, your child's skill level will be very basic. Don't worry, however; by the time she's five she'll be able to follow directions and understand some rules of a game.

Activity 1: Throwing and Catching

The catching and throwing skills of a two-year-old are very rudimentary. You'll have to stand quite close to your child to catch and throw things, although he can roll a ball back and forth between you without much trouble. He'll play more easily with larger balls, such as kickballs and beach balls (since these don't weigh very much). He'll be able to kick if he's standing still, and he'll be thrilled if you kick the ball back to him.

Activity 2: Tag

Your two-year-old is not quite ready for Hide and Seek, but she will enjoy chasing you and then letting you chase her. She won't understand the concept of being "It" and she may not be ready to take turns, since whatever part of the game she enjoys most (chasing or being chased) is what she'll want to do over and over.

Activity 3: Jumping

Your two-year-old won't be able to jump very high, but if you put something small on the ground (like a stick) and let her jump over it, or if you jump and have her mimic you, she'll enjoy the activity. Jumping is a good skill for a two-year-old to practice, because it improves strength and balance while building bone density.

Trucks

Lots of two-year-olds are fascinated by all aspects of trucks—their size, their noise, and their power. Many communities actually have annual days when the town's trucks (dump-trucks, bulldozers, etc.) line up in a parking lot so children can look at—and perhaps even climb into—the trucks. You can call your local public-works agency to find out if your town sponsors these events.

Activity 1: Pretending to Drive

If you're in the house with your truck-loving child, you can build a "truck" with a pillow or large box and have your child hold a paper plate as the steering wheel. Pull the "truck" around making honking and braking noises. (This truck can also be a car, a train, or a plane.)

Activity 2: Visiting a Construction Site

When you're trying to find something to do with your two-year-old one afternoon, don't rule out taking a drive or a walk to a local construction site. It may not sound to you like a fun place to visit, but your child will enjoy watching the people working on their trucks and laying concrete, smoothing out tar, or mixing cement. Don't forget to bring a hat and sunscreen since construction workers are usually working under bright sun!

Activity 3: Draw a Street Map

Get a piece of butcher-block paper or a large piece of newsprint, and draw a road map. Be sure to draw buildings, stop signs, and traffic and street lights on it. Your child can use this as a place to roll his cars and set down his playhouses or blocks. Once you draw straight lines and curved roads on it, he may want to draw landmarks like trees and houses.

Playing House

Two-year-olds don't do a lot of imaginative play, but they do enjoy pretend play. The two styles are similar but not exactly alike. Here's the difference: Two-year-olds pretend to be a mom, a dad, or a baby, but they don't create elaborate story lines to accompany who they are pretending to be. Once they are four or five years old, children make up entire plots and weave fantasies about the characters they are pretending to be. Until then their play is limited to mimicking and imitating people they know, including parents, other family members, teachers, and friends.

Playing Kitchen

Since child-sized kitchen sets can be expensive, you can take large cardboard boxes and paint on the details of an oven, stove, and refrigerator. Give your child pots, pans, and plastic or paper dishes so he can cook and serve dinner. His pretending won't go much further than stirring and serving a meal, so you may need to encourage him by setting up the story and adding words to the play. For example: "Oh, are you making me dinner?" "What did you make?" "Mmmm. It's good. Thank you." Ask your child questions about the meal, but if she can't tell you what she's pretending, then keep a running commentary going about the play.

Bedtime

Even if your two-year-old doesn't have a toy crib or cradle, you can use a box for a bed and let your toddler put a doll or stuffed animal to bed. You might give him all the objects you use when you put him to bed, such as a toothbrush and toothpaste, washcloth, sheets for the bed (you can use dish-towels), some books, and a stuffed animal for the "baby." This is a good game to play with a toddler who doesn't like to go to bed himself.

Telling a Story

Many parents think there is a trick to telling a good story, but all popular stories have one thing in common—one of a limited number of basic plot lines. In other words, great children's stories follow similar paths.

Plot Event	Two-Year-Old Version
Boy wants girl	Princess wants to find a new kitten/young pirate wants to find treasure
Boy tries to win girl	Princess searches castle/ young pirate sets out to sea
Boy gets girl	Princess sees a kitten/ young pirate finds an island
Boy loses girl	Kitten hides from princess/ pirate can't swim to island
Boy strives to get girl again	Princess bakes a special cake that gets the kitten to trust her/pirate is brave enough to swim to the island
Boy gets girl	Kitten licks the princess/ pirate gets the treasure

You can use these formats with virtually any type of character. To create new variations, have the heroes or heroines set different goals or meet different fates in their quest. Try to make the stories you tell relevant to your particular audience. If your two-year-old is afraid of water, have him be a pirate who has to swim to an island to get the treasure. If your little princess wants a kitten, tell her a story about taking care of a cat. If you stick to this basic outline, you'll tell an exciting story no matter what its ending.

Appendix B

Toddler Health and Developmental Information

If you're looking for further information on medical and developmental issues that might concern two-year-olds, here's an annotated guide to reliable books and Web sites for parents. If you ever find yourself in what feels like a "this can't be happening to me" power struggle with your child, picking up one of these books will reassure you that you're not the first parent (nor will you be the last) to come up against an independent toddler.

Toddler Development Books

Having realistic expectations of the processes by which your child is growing up is helpful for ignoring some behaviors. These books explain what all children go through as they learn and develop, which makes it easier for parents to accept the realities of two-year-old behavior.

The Girlfriends' Guide to Toddlers: A Survival Manual to the Terrible Twos (and Ones and Threes) From the First Step, the First Potty and the First Word (No) to the Last Blankie. **Vicki Iovine (Penguin Group, January 1999)**
This fun and easy-to-read book is reassuring to all moms. It points out that everything you'll deal with as a parent is something your most honest and trustworthy girlfriends will also go through.

How to Talk so Your Child will Listen and Listen so Your Child will Talk. **Adele Faber (Harper Collins, 2004)**
This is an important book for convincing parents of young children that if you build a relationship that allows your child to feel safe and important, he might continue to talk and be open with you as he grows up. The steps in this book are easy to follow and make a lot of sense.

To Listen to a Child: Understanding the Normal Problems of Growing Up. **T. Berry Brazelton (Addison-Wesley, 1991)**
This book reassures parents that many of the phases their children go through are not only normal, but also impor-

tant developmental milestones. Many parents these days worry that a problem will follow their child into adulthood. But learning good parenting techniques allows you to help your child grow through and beyond each phase, whether it be bed-wetting, lying, stealing, or fearfulness. Understanding the developmental process helps parents put their child's stages in perspective so as to deal with them more effectively.

Toddler Development Web Sites

Some of these Web sites have bulletin boards and helpful articles, including ideas contributed by parents on how to help your child sleep, eat, and behave better.

www.parenting.com
From *Parenting* magazine, this Web site includes archived articles on age-specific subjects, broken down by health, nutrition, and other categories. Information is very detailed. You can read, for example, "Backpack Ready Baby" and "Look Who's Walking!" Includes separate articles for mothers. You can also access this site through *www.parenting.aol.com*.

www.child.com
This site has short, informative articles as well as timely stories. It is much more like a traditional magazine than others. Includes cultural information (such as "The Ten Best Museums for Kids") and a "Daily Laugh," as well as health, wellness, and developmental items.

www.ivillage.com

Click on the parenting tab, then locate the age of your child to read more on a range of issues. Included are reliable health information, quizzes, nutrition and recipes, as well as shopping info and crafts. Some information comes from magazines associated with iVillage, including *Good Housekeeping* and *Redbook*.

Toddler Health Web Sites

If you ever have specific medical questions about your child, you can go to these Web sites to learn more about symptoms and what your doctor will look for and prescribe for illnesses.

www.autism-society.org

If you have concerns about your child and autism, speak to your doctor. Beware of personal Web pages and blogs that might frighten you about autism. Instead, look for reliable information, and don't panic before you've gotten a diagnosis that sounds reasonable to you. This Web site gives detailed information about the range of autism diagnoses. It includes health information and support, and works to raise funds to help children with these challenges.

www.aafa.org

This is the official site of the Asthma and Allergy Foundation of America and offers a wealth of information about the symptoms and treatments of these illnesses. It gives you help on locating the right physician as well as information for helping your child cope with allergies.

www.webmd.com

This site is full of helpful information for people of all ages, but you can go to its "parenting and family" page for extensive facts and advice on a wide variety of childhood illnesses and behavioral issues. There are physician and parent blogs, as well as Q & As and a "Symptom Checker" page.

www.aap.org

This is the Web site of the American Academy of Pediatrics and is designed for both parents and doctors. You can search for highly reliable health information by age or topic. Even though it is written in a dry manner, it's altogether a valuable resource for health information.

Toddler Health Books

You can consult these books for information on symptoms, including what your doctor looks for when diagnosing illness, and common prescriptions.

Dr. Spock's Baby and Child Care. **Benjamin Spock (Simon & Schuster Adult Publishing Group, June 2004)**

An updated version of the classic book offers reliable, easy-to-understand advice and explanations about the behavior of your child.

The Irreducible Needs of Children: What Every Child Must Have to Grow, Learn, and Flourish. **T. Berry Brazleton (Perseus Publishing, 2000)**

This is a book that emphasizes the importance of nurturing a child's development and spirit. Rather than focusing on "Don'ts," this book explains what types of behavior and teaching help a child grow and develop.

American Medical Association Complete Guide to Your Children's Health. **D. Kotulak (New York: Random House, 1999)**

This encyclopedia of health information will help you deal with illness, as well as explain what your doctor is thinking and considering when he sees your child.

The Optimistic Child. Martin Seligman **(HarperCollins, 1996)**

Seligman, one of the first psychologists to study happiness and positivity, explores and explains ways to help your child feel good about himself. The program isn't touchy-feely but rather involves mastering skills and appreciating accomplishments. It's very down-to-earth.

General Toddler Web Sites

These Web sites are not meant for your children to look at, but are instead offered for you to find out more about activities and answers to questions.

www.familyfun.com

This is the Web site to go to for crafts, activities, and creative ideas, as well as timely recipes (for holidays) and birthday party ideas. Also useful for vacation suggestions.

www.tvturnoff.org

If you struggle with turning off the TV in your house because you wonder what to do with your children once it's not on, or because the other adults in your household don't support you, try this site. It will give you reasons to turn the TV off, ideas on what to do once it's off, and other helpful information.

www.nationalgeographic.com/kids

This site offers information on animals, science, and weather, helping you answer your child's questions. You might also be inspired by activities to do outdoors.

www.preschooleducation.com

This is not a "find a preschool" site, but rather one that offers preschool teachers helpful information on lessons and activities. You'll find information a parent can use and appreciate. It includes printable coloring pages.

www.drspock.com

This Web site has excellent articles, including some on how to find a preschool, as well as reliable medical and behavioral information.

www.naeyc.org

The National Association for the Education of Young Children (NAEYC), a respected nonprofit organization, has long been a leader in high-quality early-childhood education. It maintains a regularly updated online listing of accredited preschool programs.

Safety Web Sites

Though most adults feel fairly safe in the world, keeping children safe involves learning specific skills and getting appropriate information. If you learn some basic skills, for example, how to install a car seat, chances are your child will grow up with just a few scratches.

www.ada.org

If you have questions about how to help your child not be afraid of the dentist or if you would like to find a dentist who specializes in helping small children, go to this site, which is the official online location of the American Dental Association.

www.car-safety.org

All you need to make sure your car seat is installed properly and to choose the seat that is right for your car. This site will also help you find an expert to check your seat's installation.

www.healthytransportation.net

This site explains how transportation accidents are likely to happen and what parents can do to prevent them. Using the site for background and how-to information will reassure you when you strap your child in for an outing.

Appendix C

Books and Toys for Two-Year-Olds

Books

Most of the books on this list are classics, written and illustrated by renowned authors and artists. You are sure to find volumes that you and your children will love. The list includes a few books by Eric Carle, a well-known writer and illustrator of more than seventy children's books. You can visit the Eric Carle Museum of Picture Book Art in Amherst, Massachusetts with your two-year-old. Go to *www.picturebookart.org* to learn more.

Are You My Mother? by P.D. Eastman (Random House Books for Young Readers)

Balls! (Sesame Street Elmo's World) by John E. Barrett (Random House Books for Young Readers)

Bear Likes to Play in the Sunshine by Stella Blackstone and Debbie Harter (Barefoot Books)

Brown Bear, Brown Bear, What Do You See? by Bill Martin Jr. and Eric Carle (Henry Holt & Co.)

Chicka Chicka Boom Boom by Bill Martin Jr. (Aladdin Picture Books)

Clifford the Big Red Dog by Norman Bridwell (Cartwheel)

Curious George by H.A. and Margret Rey (Houghton Mifflin)

Don't Let The Pigeon Stay Up Late by Mo Willems (Hyperion)

Dr. Seuss's ABC: An Amazing Alphabet Book! by Dr. Seuss (Random House Books for Young Readers)

Frog and Toad Are Friends by Arnold Lobel (HarperTrophy)

Go Dog Go by P. D. Eastman (Random House Books for Young Readers)

Goodnight Moon by Margaret Wise Brown and Clement Hurd (HarperFestival)

Guess How Much I Love You by Sam McBratney (Candlewick)

Harold and the Purple Crayon by Crockett Johnson (HarperCollins)

Hop on Pop by Dr. Seuss (Random House Books for Young Readers)

If You Give a Mouse a Cookie by Laura Joffe Numeroffe (Laura Geringer)

Knuffle Bunny: A Cautionary Tale by Mo Willems (Hyperion)

Make Way for Ducklings by Robert McCloskey (Viking Juvenile)

Moo Baa La La by Sandra Boynton (Little Simon)

Mr. Brown Can Moo, Can You?: Dr. Seuss's Book of Wonderful Noises by Dr. Seuss (Random House Books for Young Readers)

Pat the Bunny by Dorothy Kunhardt (Golden Books)

Polar Bear, Polar Bear What Do You See? by Bill Martin Jr. and Eric Carle (Henry Holt & Co.)

Quiet Loud by Leslie Petricelli (Candlewick)

The Carrot Seed by Ruth Krauss and Crockett Johnson (HarperCollins)

The Mitten by Alvin Tresselt (HarperTrophy)

The Napping House by Audrey and Don Wood (Red Wagon Books)

The Rainbow Fish by Marcus Pfister (North-South)

The Runaway Bunny by Margaret Wise Brown and Clement Hurd (HarperFestival)

The Very Hungry Caterpillar by Eric Carle (Philomel)

Where Is Baby's Belly Button? By Karen Katz (Little Simon)

Where the Wild Things Are by Maurice Sendak (HarperCollins)

Toys

When it comes to buying toys for toddlers, there are a few things to keep in mind. First, if it looks cheap or is in fact cheap, it's not worth any price you pay for it, because cheaply made toys break easily. The best way to choose toys is by brand and by the quality of the store. Toys "R" Us and Target, as well as small, privately owned toy stores, usually carry brands that are durable and well made.

Dolls and stuffed animals are perhaps the most beloved toys of both boys and girls. A doll gives a two-year-old someone to care for, love, and play with. Toys "R" Us has a large selection of Cabbage Patch and other baby dolls.

Toys for Pretending

Two-year-olds especially love toys that help them pretend. Your two-year-old may enjoy:

- Dollhouses
- Toy fire stations
- Playmobil's Farm Starter Set, which comes with animals, a barn, and a farm family.
- Little Helpers' Complete Compact Kitchen with Microwave Oven, Dishwasher, Sink, Stove, Refrigerator, and Phone
- Little Doctor Kit by I-Play Outdoors
- Little Builder Tool Belt by I-Play Outdoors

Many of the newer pretend toys have built-in sounds, but keep in mind that children love to make their own noises. Look for quiet "pretend" toys. This will save your own nerves while still encouraging your child to play.

Toys for Movement

Two-year-olds like to move fast, so toys that move, like tricycles and wagons, are especially fun for them.

- Preschool Scooter by Huffy Sports
- ATW Cargo Wagon by Radio Flyer

Toy Vehicles

Most young children love trucks, trains, and other vehicles. Even if they don't pretend to drive them, they will dump and move sand and dirt to create play spaces for their toys and dolls. Some vehicle toys your two-year-old might enjoy are:

- Tonka's Trencher Backhoe
- Tonka's Bulldozer
- Tonka's Mighty Loader
- Manhattan Toy Company's Rumblies Danny Dump Truck
- Geo Trax Working Town Railway System and other train sets

Blocks

Blocks are a must for two-year-olds. Besides the basic brown wooden shapes, try:

- First Blocks by Haba
- Oversized Lego-style blocks, such as the 250-Piece Mini Tub by Mega Bloks

One must-name brand of toys for young kids is Melissa & Doug. This company makes gorgeous puzzles and blocks, including:

- Classic Wooden Geometric Stacker
- Large Wooden Geometric Shapes
- Jumbo Knob 8-piece Puzzle
- Deluxe 50-piece Wooden ABC/123 Blocks Set
- Wooden Take-Along 24-piece Tool Kit

Crafts and Sports

If your two-year-old enjoys arts and crafts, consider purchasing one of the following, both of which encourage drawing, painting, and gluing:

- An easel or large art table
- The Creative Art Center with Folding Chair by Step2

For your little athlete, try the following. They allow two-year-olds to throw basketballs into hoops, get a hole in one, and play just like a grown-up.

- Easy Score Basketball Set by Little Tikes
- Golf Games by Little Tikes

Beads and Blocks on Wires

Beads and blocks on wires allow two-year-olds to move small pieces without losing them. Two of the best of these toys are:

- 5-way Giant Bead Maze by Imaginarium
- Busy Ball Popper by Hasbro

Index